Central Baptist Association of Nova Scotia

Minutes of the 21. Session of the Central Baptist Association of

Nova Scotia

Held With the Fifth Cornwallis Church, Pereaux

Central Baptist Association of Nova Scotia

Minutes of the 21. Session of the Central Baptist Association of Nova Scotia
Held With the Fifth Cornwallis Church, Pereaux

ISBN/EAN: 9783743614161

Printed in Europe, USA, Canada, Australia, Japan.

Cover: Foto ©ninafisch / pixelio.de

Manufactured and distributed by brebook publishing software
(www.brebook.com)

Central Baptist Association of Nova Scotia

Minutes of the 21. Session of the Central Baptist Association of Nova Scotia

Technical and Bibliographic Notes/Notes techniques et bibliographiques

The Institute has attempted to obtain the best original copy available for filming. Features of this copy which may be bibliographically unique, which may alter any of the images in the reproduction, or which may significantly change the usual method of filming, are checked below.

L'Institut a microfilmé le meilleur exemplaire qu'il lui a été possible de se procurer. Les détails de cet exemplaire qui sont peut-être uniques du point de vue bibliographique, qui peuvent modifier une image reproduite, ou qui peuvent exiger une modification dans la méthode normale de filmage sont indiqués ci-dessous.

- [ ] Coloured covers/
  Couverture de couleur

- [ ] Covers damaged/
  Couverture endommagée

- [ ] Covers restored and/or laminated/
  Couverture restaurée et/ou pelliculée

- [ ] Cover title missing/
  Le titre de couverture manque

- [ ] Coloured maps/
  Cartes géographiques en couleur

- [ ] Coloured ink (i.e. other than blue or black)/
  Encre de couleur (i.e. autre que bleue ou noire)

- [ ] Coloured plates and/or illustrations/
  Planches et/ou illustrations en couleur

- [x] Bound with other material/
  Relié avec d'autres documents

- [x] Tight binding may cause shadows or distortion along interior margin/
  La reliure serrée peut causer de l'ombre ou de la distortion le long de la marge intérieure

- [ ] Blank leaves added during restoration may appear within the text. Whenever possible, these have been omitted from filming/
  Il se peut que certaines pages blanches ajoutées lors d'une restauration apparaissent dans le texte, mais, lorsque cela était possible, ces pages n'ont pas été filmées.

- [ ] Additional comments:/
  Commentaires supplémentaires:

- [ ] Coloured pages/
  Pages de couleur

- [ ] Pages damaged/
  Pages endommagées

- [ ] Pages restored and/or laminated/
  Pages restaurées et/ou pelliculées

- [ ] Pages discoloured, stained or foxed/
  Pages décolorées, tachetées ou piquées

- [ ] Pages detached/
  Pages détachées

- [x] Showthrough/
  Transparence

- [ ] Quality of print varies/
  Qualité inégale de l'impression

- [ ] Includes supplementary material/
  Comprend du matériel supplémentaire

- [ ] Only edition available/
  Seule édition disponible

- [ ] Pages wholly or partially obscured by errata slips, tissues, etc., have been refilmed to ensure the best possible image/
  Les pages totalement ou partiellement obscurcies par un feuillet d'errata, une pelure, etc., ont été filmées à nouveau de façon à obtenir la meilleure image possible.

- [ ] This item is filmed at the reduction ratio checked below/
  Ce document est filmé au taux de réduction indiqué ci-dessous.

The copy filmed here has been reproduced thanks to the generosity of:

Harold Campbell Vaughan Memorial Library
Acadia University

The images appearing here are the best quality possible considering the condition and legibility of the original copy and in keeping with the filming contract specifications.

Original copies in printed paper covers are filmed beginning with the front cover and ending on the last page with a printed or illustrated impression, or the back cover when appropriate. All other original copies are filmed beginning on the first page with a printed or illustrated impression, and ending on the last page with a printed or illustrated impression.

The last recorded frame on each microfiche shall contain the symbol —▶ (meaning "CONTINUED"), or the symbol ▽ (meaning "END"), whichever applies.

Maps, plates, charts, etc., may be filmed at different reduction ratios. Those too large to be entirely included in one exposure are filmed beginning in the upper left hand corner, left to right and top to bottom, as many frames as required. The following diagrams illustrate the method:

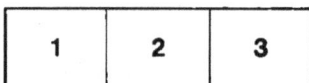

L'exemplaire filmé fut reproduit grâce à la générosité de:

Harold Campbell Vaughan Memorial Library
Acadia University

Les images suivantes ont été reproduites avec le plus grand soin, compte tenu de la condition et de la netteté de l'exemplaire filmé, et en conformité avec les conditions du contrat de filmage.

Les exemplaires originaux dont la couverture en papier est imprimée sont filmés en commençant par le premier plat et en terminant soit par la dernière page qui comporte une empreinte d'impression ou d'illustration, soit par le second plat, selon le cas. Tous les autres exemplaires originaux sont filmés en commençant par la première page qui comporte une empreinte d'impression ou d'illustration et en terminant par la dernière page qui comporte une telle empreinte.

Un des symboles suivants apparaîtra sur la dernière image de chaque microfiche, selon le cas: le symbole —▶ signifie "A SUIVRE", le symbole ▽ signifie "FIN".

Les cartes, planches, tableaux, etc., peuvent être filmés à des taux de réduction différents. Lorsque le document est trop grand pour être reproduit en un seul cliché, il est filmé à partir de l'angle supérieur gauche, de gauche à droite, et de haut en bas, en prenant le nombre d'images nécessaire. Les diagrammes suivants illustrent la méthode.

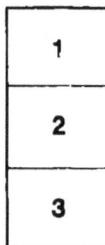

1	2	3

1
2
3

𝔅

FIFTE

Saturday,

CI

Nova S

" CII

MINUTES

OF THE

Twenty-First Session

OF THE

CENTRAL
Baptist Association,

OF

NOVA SCOTIA,

HELD WITH THE

FIFTH CORNWALLIS CHURCH, PEREAUX,

Saturday, Monday, Tuesday, June 24th, 26th, 27th, 1871.

TOGETHER WITH THE

CIRCULAR LETTER,

AND REPORT OF

Nova Scotia Baptist Home Missionary Society.

"CHRISTIAN MESSENGER" OFFICE,
HALIFAX. N. S.
1871.

the 5il
In t.
tion wa
of the
Whil
Associn
The l

Upper
Beriah Gi
Bridgew
Chelsea,-
Chester,-
Cornwall.
Harris, Wi
Cornwalli
Pineo, Wm.
Cornwalli
Brothers Ja
Cornwallis
Brethren Al
Canning, (
worth, Edwi
Falmouth.—
Etter.
Halifax 1st
Rand, R. N.
Halifax 2nd
W. Clark.
Hammond's
Hantsport.—
West.
Horton 1st.—
Deacon Faulki
Horton 2nd.-
Jehiel Coldwell
Horton 3rd.—
Indian Harbor
Jeddore.—Rev
Kempt.—Rev.
Lahave.—Rev
Maitland.—R
New Cornwall.

New Germany.—Rev. W. F. Hall.

Newport West.—Deacon Edward Masters, and James E. Nelson.

Rawdon.—Brethren John McLearn, and Richard McLearn.

Sackville.—Deacon Francis Webber.

St. Margaret's Bay.—Rev. T. C. Delong.

Windsor.—Rev. D. M. Welton, A. M. ‹

Western Association.—Revds. W. G. Parker, J. M. Parker, and G. D. Cox.

The ballot being taken the Rev. E. O. Read was duly elected *Moderator* for the ensuing year.

Secretary, Rev. S. March.

Assistant Secretary, Rev. W. F. Hall.

Treasurer, W. C. Bill.

Assistant Treasurer, Edwin Rand.

The following Committees were appointed :—

To EXAMINE LETTERS.—Revds. Geo. Weathers, W. G. Parker, and T. C. Delong.

To READ LETTERS.—Revds. S. W. DeBlois, Joseph Murray, and Deacon Judge McCully.

ON NOMINATION AND ARRANGEMENTS.—Revds. D. Freeman, James Parker, S. B. Kempton ; Brethren Edwin Rand, D. H. Newcomb, James Bligh, and D. F. Higgins.

The following Brethren were invited to a seat :—

Rev. T. A. Higgins, A. M., Brethren C. F. Eaton, Ed. Beckwith, John Vaughan, Philip Hamilton, Henry Thomas, Bro. W. Bradshaw, (Lic.) P. E. L. Caleb Burgess, Rufus Sanford, (Lic.), Wm. North, Revds. John Chase, and James Newcomb.

The Committee proceeded to read the letters from the Churches.

The Committee of Arrangements presented in part their Report as follows :—

That there be a Prayer-meeting each morning at 6 o'clock in this house.

That the Morning Sessions begin at 10 o'clock, and close at 12½ o'clock, P. M. That the Afternoon Session begin at 12 ½ o'clock, P. M., and close at 6 o'clock, P. M.

That all Committees meet on Monday morning at 9 o'clock, A.M.

That the Report on Missions be presented on Monday at 2½ o'clock, P. M., at which time the Association allow the Home Mission Society to hold its Annual Meeting.

That other Reports be presented on Monday at 6 o'clock, P. M.

That the Report on Education be presented on Tuesday at 10 o'clock, A. M.

SABBATH SERVICES.

Pereaux,—Rev. S. March, at 11 a. m.; Rev. Joseph Murray, at 7 p. m.

Canning,—Rev. J. M. Cramp, D. D., at 11 a. m.; Rev. S. March, at 3 ½ p. m.; Rev. E. M. Saunders, at 7 P. M.

Methodist Church, Canning,—Rev. J. E. Goucher, at 11 a. m.

Congregationalist Church, Habitant,—Rev. S. T. Rand, at 11 a. m.

Free Baptist Church, Habitant,—Rev. J. L. Read, at 11 a. m.
Lower Pereaux,—Rev. George Weathers, at 11 a. m., and 3 p. m.
Scot's Bay Road,—Rev. J. Thomas, at 11 a. m., and 3 p. m.
Scot's Bay,—Rev. J. M. Parker, at 11 a. m., and 6 p. m.
Woodworth Mountain,—Rev. J. Meadows, at 11 a. m., and 7 p. m
West Mountain,—Brother Bradshaw, at 3 p. m.
Woodside,—Rev. T. S. Delong, at 8 p. m.
Medford,—Rev. Robert Philp, at 4 p. m.
Canard,—Rev. D. M. Welton, at 11 a. m.
Billtown,—Rev. E. O. Read, at 11 a. m.
Kentville,—Rev. W. G. Parker, at 3 p. m.
Gaspereaux,—Rev. W. E. Hall.

Report adopted.
Prayer by Rev . Cramp.
Adjourned to meet at 2 ½ o'clock, P. M.

Afternoon Session, June 24th.

Association resumed its 2 ½ o'clock, P. M., by singing, and prayer by Rev. J. E. Goucher.

The Minutes of the Morning Session were read and approved.

Reading of Letters from the Churches was resumed.

The Committee of Arrangements presented a further Report :—

COMMITTEES.

To Examine the Circular Letter.—Revds. J. E. Goucher and Joseph Murray, and Brother J. Bligh.

The Christian Messenger.—Hon. J. McCully, Revds. J. Parker, D. Freeman, S. DeBlois, Joshua Ells, L. C. Woodworth, J. Murray, J. L. Read, S. B. Kempten, W. G. Parker, D. M. Welton, S. March.

Benevolent Funds.—Revds. E. M. Saunders, D. M. Welton, Brethren Wm. Rusco, Francis Webber, A. W. Clark, Edwin Rand, C. F. Eaton, and W. M. Sandford.

Education.—Revds. J. M. Cramp, D. D., Dr. Sawyer, D. F. Higgins, Albert Coldwell; Deacons T. H. Rand, Bacon, Ed. Parker, Faulkner.

Missions.—Revds. I. J. Skinner, T. C. Delong, J. Meadows, Brethren Wm. H. Webster, George Weathers, A. A. Pineo, A. D. Shaw, John Thomas.

Questions on Letters.—Revds. R. Philp; Dr. Cramp, D. M. Welton, Brethren Shubael Dimock, Oliver Cogswell, S. Selden, and Hon J. McCully.

Obituaries.—Revds. S. B. Kempton, E. M. Saunders, J. L. Read, Charles E. Parker.

Report adopted.

An interesting discussion took place in reference to the Statistics of Sabbath Schools in which a number of brethren took part.

Resolved, That the Secretary of the Association be instructed to forward a copy of the Statistics of Sabbath Schools in this Association to the Sabbath School Convention. Passed.

Resolved, That any ministers of this Association visiting the Western Association be our delegates to that body. Passed.

Resolved, That Rev. T. A. Higgins and Bro. S. Selden, and any other three brethren, members of this body, visiting the Eastern Association be our delegates to that Association. Passed.

Resolved, That the following brethren be our delegates to the Convention ; Hon. Judge McCully, A. A. Pineo, Francis Webber, Edward Parker, and T. H. Rand. Passed.

Resolved, that 1000 copies of the Minutes of this Association be printed as last year, by Bro. Selden, and that 50 copies be reserved for the Association, and paid for at the same rate. Passed.

The Rev. Dr. Cramp, in accordance with a notice given last year, that the first article of the Constitution of this Association be amended by inserting the words, " not exceeding five from any one Association," immediately after the words " together with delegates from Corresponding Associations." Passed.

Hon. Judge McCully, Chairman of Committee appointed to apply to the Legislature for an Act to enable Baptist Churches to perpetuate Trustees ; presented a verbal report, whereupon it was moved that said Committee be continued in office. Passed.

After prayer by Rev. D. M. Welton, A. M., Association adjourned to meet again on Monday morning at 10 o'clock.

Monday Morning Session, June 26th.

The Introductory Sermon was preached by Rev. J. E. Goucher of Halifax, from 1 Thess. iii. 8. Subject :—"The steadfastness of the Church, the evidence and support of a living ministry."

Prayer by Rev. W. G. Parker.

The remaining Letters from churches were read.

The Committee on Circular Letter presented their Report, recommending that the said letter be read. It was accordingly read by the writer, Rev. S. W. DeBlois, A. M.

Resolved, That the letter now read be adopted and printed with the Minutes, and that the Editor of the " *Christian Messenger*" be respectfully requested to publish the same in that paper. Passed.

Resolved, That the Rev. J. E. Goucher be requested to furnish a copy of the excellent Introductory Sermon to which we have listened and forward it to the " *Christian Messenger*" for insertion in its columns.

REPORT UPON THE " CHRISTIAN MESSENGER."

The Report of the Committee on the " *Christian Messenger*" was presented and adopted.

It having been the practice to have a Committee upon

the subject of the *Christian Messenger*, and a Report prepared annually for adoption at each recurring Association, the following is submitted as containing the views of the Committee appointed during the present Session.

The *Christian Messenger* has heretofore and hitherto proved itself an invaluable auxilliary for the promotion of evangelical objects in connection with our denomination. While its readers have at the same time been supplied with a large amount of useful secular information, and the current news of the day. Your Committee therefore recommend it to the warmest sympathies of Baptist families and Baptist Churches. No higher or better guarantee for its future management, while under the control of it present Editor, is, in the opinion of your Committee, required, than a reference to its past history.

Under these circumstances it would scarcely seem to be necessary at each succeeding Association to appoint a Committee with a view of recording an expression of opinion upon the subject of its merits or its management.

All which is respectfully submitted.

J. McCULLY, *Chairman.*

Pereaux, June 26th, 1871.

Prayer by Rev. S. T. Rand.
Adjourned until 2½, P. M.

Afternoon Session, June 26th.

Singing, and prayer by Rev. A. W. Sawyer, D. D.

Voted, That Rev. I. J. Skinner be Chairman of the Committee on Missions.

The Report of the Treasurer of the Infirm Ministers' Fund was presented and adopted. (See Appendix A.)

Voted, That the Board of the Infirm Minister's Fund be re-appointed, substituting the name of Bro. Edward Beckwith, for that of Mayhew Beckwith, Esq., deceased.

Voted, That the Association do now adjourn to allow the Home Missionary Society to hold its Annual Meeting.

The Annual Session of the N. S. Home Missionary Society was held, and the Officers and Board of Managers for the ensuing year elected. Good speeches were made in setting forth the claims of Home Missions on the churches.

Prayer by Rev. I. J. Skinner.

The business of the Association again resumed.
Prayer by Rev. James Parker.
The Committee on Questions in Letters presented their Report.

Voted, That the Report be taken up clause by clause. After considerable discussion on the first clause, it was unanimously adopted. Second clause passed unanimously.

That the letters received from the African Baptist Churches at Halifax and Hammond's Plains, asking for admission into this Association, not containing sufficient information as to the reason why they seceded from the organization known as the African Baptist Association. We therefore recommend that a Committee be appointed to enquire into the merits of the case and report at the first session of the next Association.

They also recommend that our next Association be held with the 2nd Cornwallis Church, at Berwick.

R. R. PHILP, *Chairman*.

In accordance with the above Report the following Committee was appointed, viz., Revs. J. M. Cramp, D. D., James Parker, J. E. Goucher, E. M. Saunders, David Shaw, T. C. Delong and Deacon David Thompson :—

Voted, That the Treasurer of this Association be instructed to pay over the moneys in his hands, to the Treasurers of the various Boards for which they are designated.

Voted, That Rev. D. Freeman, A. M., preach the Associational Sermon next year, and that Rev. I. J. Skinner be his alternate.

Voted, That Rev. T. A. Higgins write the Circular Letter.

Voted, That any two members of this Association visiting the Prince Edward Island Association be our delegates to that body.

Voted, That the church at Waterville be retained on the Minutes for another year; Brethren D. M. Welton, and I. J. Skinner having requested its continuance and engaging to enquire into its standing, and report next year.

Voted, That the Burton Church be also retained at the request of Brethren S. Selden, and F. Webber, they also agreeing to make enquiry concerning it and report next year.

Voted, That Brethren S. Selden, A. Clarke, Revs. O. E. Read and A. A. Pineo be a Committee to make arrangements with the proper authorities, for the usual reduction in Railway fares to those in attendance at the Central Association, at Berwick next year.

Voted, That the Ministers be requested to read from their pulpits the Circular Letter from this body to the churches.

Hon. Judge McCully delivered an eloquent address in favor of Female Education, Ministerial Culture, and Benevolence.

After prayer by Rev. J. L. Read, the Association adjourned to meet to-morrow morning, at 10 o'clock.

Tuesday Morning Session, June 27th.

The Moderator in the chair. Meeting opened by singing the 23rd Hymn, and prayer by Rev. S. B. Kempton.

Committee on Missions reported. Report laid on the table.

Minutes of last Session read and adopted.

Letter read from the Burton Church, (African.)

Voted, That the Committee appointed to enquire and report concerning said church be relieved from the duty imposed upon them by the resolution of yesterday.

Report on Missions taken up. Addresses by Bro S. Selden, Revs. E. M. Saunders, S. T. Rand, S. B. Kempton, and D. Freeman. Report adopted. (See Appendix B.)

Committee on Education presented their report.

Deeply interesting addresses were delivered on this subject by Revs. D. Freeman, Dr. Sawyer, D. M. Welton, G. D. Cox, Jas. Parker, and Bro. Rufus Sandford. Report adopted. (See Appendix C.)

The Committee on Obituaries reported. Report recommitted for completion, and ordered to be printed with the minutes. (See Appendix D.)

The Committee on Benevolent Funds reported. Report adopted. See Appendix E.)

The time was extended for one hour.

Bro. T. H. Rand moved the following Resolution, seconded by Prof. D. F. Higgins, which passed unanimously.

Whereas, The erection of buildings for a Male and Female Seminary, and also for our College Library and Museum in connection with our Institutions at Horton is an immediate necessity, the entire cost of which would probably be about $25,000 :

Therefore Resolved, That it be recommended to the Board of Governors of Acadia College to divide the same in shares of $250. each, and the benevolent of the denomination be solicited to take one or more of these shares till the whole are taken up.

Voted, That the Revs. E. M. Saunders, J. E. Goucher, and Bro. S. Selden be requested to prepare an Abstract of the Letters from the churches for publication in the *Christian Messenger.*

Voted, That the thanks of this Association be presented to the brethren, sisters, and friends, of the fifth Cornwallis Church, and vicinity, for their kindness and hospitality during the present Session.

Voted, That we adjourn to meet with the Second Cornwallis Church, Berwick, on the first Saturday after the 20th of June, 1872, at 10 o'clock, A. M.

Singing, and prayer by Rev. Dr. Cramp.

Benediction by Moderator.

E. O. READ, *Moderator.*

STEPHEN MARCH, *Secretary.*

WM. E. HALL, *Assistant Secretary.*

Circular Letter.

THE CIRCULAR LETTER FROM THE NOVA SCOTIA CENTRAL BAPTIST ASSOCIATION TO THE CHURCHES OF WHICH IT IS COMPOSED.

Dear Brethren,—

We propose on this occasion to present before you some thoughts in relation to the Lord's Supper, an ordinance of the Church of God of no mean importance.

There are four passages in the New Testament which give an account of the origin of this rite. Mat. xxvi. 26-29. Mark xiv. 22-25. Luke xxii. 19-20. 1 Cor. xi. 23-26. By examining these, which agree substantially, we shall get all the information (save from incidental allusions) that is contained in the Word of God. From these we may learn. I. What the ordinance is not. II. What it is. III. What class of persons is entitled to participate therein. IV. The duties enjoined upon those who partake.

I. This ordinance, is *not* a sacrifice for sin. Christ was *once* offered and requires not that sacrifices of himself should again and again be made. We need scarcely advert to the absurd and unscriptural notions, by which the Church of Rome, and other Churches, so called, under pretence of exalting the mystery, pervert and destroy the original idea of the institution. The words " This is my body " so plainly figurative, being alleged in support of the theory, that the bread and wine are changed into the actual body and blood of Christ. No one can pretend to misunderstand our Lord, when he says " I am the door," " I am the way," " I am the vine."

The Communion is not a way or method of salvation.— Those who are anxious about their souls, are frequently encouraged to come to the Lord's table. It is hoped that the vivid representation there made, of the sufferings of Christ, and the solemnity and deep feeling,—developed by the whole ceremony, will have a tendency to draw such persons to Christ, and give them peace in believing. However plausible such a view may seem, it has no authority, either by precept or example, from the Word of God. The custom arises from a mistaken view of the ordinance, and it may be also, from an erroneous idea of the condition of mind of those, who profess to be seeking salvation.

We might advert to other theories, which have been held, and put forth on this subject, but time would fail us. We pass on to consider

II. What this rite is.

1. It is an ordinance of Divine appointment. *This do.* It was instituted by Him to whom all power is given, in heaven and on earth. It was instituted in a marked, impressive and binding manner. Thus it bears all the sanction and weight of a Divine command. With everything adapted to give force to the command, touching pathos and solemnity to the occasion, we should keep the feast, not forsaking the assembling of ourselves together, as the manner of some is, and so much the more as we see the day approaching.

2. Again, This is a Commemorative Rite. It commemorates to the world a great transaction. Leslie, in his "Short method with a Deist," makes use of this fact, as a powerful evidence of christianity. Here is a succession. No observance of the church is more distinctly and more clearly traced to the very words of Jesus, than this. Positive ordinances may have some disadvantages, in that they may be misinterpreted or perverted, but they have this benefit, that they are a standing memorial from generation to generation, that certain events took place.

Men die. Faiths change. But just so long as ordinances are observed, we have a clue by which to trace their original design.

Almost every sect which professes to be christian, celebrates this observance. The Roman Catholics it is true, have mutilated it by depriving the laity of the cup, have perverted it by exalting it in the place of Christ. The Friends or Quakers have abolished it altogether; but all others concur in commemorating to the world, the great events it is intended to betoken.

It commemorates to the church her great Head. "Do this in remembrance of me." "Ye do shew forth the Lord's death." It commemorates to the individual who receives it, a wonderful transaction in which he himself has participated. It brings before his mind, certain truths adapted both to humble, and to make him joyful. His own christian experience is involved in the celebration. He remembers the time when he came first to Jesus; when the words of love and mercy entered his heart, filling his soul with gladness and joy. The ordinance becomes indeed to him a eucharist, a glowing offering of thanksgiving and praise. "What shall I render unto the Lord for his benefits toward me? I will take the cup of salvation, and call upon the name of the Lord." I will pay my vows, which my lips have uttered when I was in trouble.

3. And this brings us to consider, thirdly that the Supper is a symbolic rite. Under the former dispensation, the method of teaching by symbols was very freely used. Thus

the Mercy Seat, the Holy of Holies, the Sacrifices, were emblems. They were very fitting in what may be termed the childhood of the human race. The picture or form of a thing, is well adapted to aid the memory and judgement of a child. But when the mind has become matured, these to a great extent can be dispensed with. When I became a man I put away childish things. Thus in the epistle to the Galatians, the Apostle speaks of the law, as poor, weak and rudimentary, but still adapted to the time and purpose, for which it was designed.

In the kingdom of Christ this teaching is almost entirely put aside. The law was our schoolmaster to bring us unto Christ, but having accepted Christ we are no longer under a schoolmaster.

In the two positive ordinances of the christian church however, and only in these it appears to have been beneficially retained.

The one, that of Baptism, symbolises the death, burial and resurrection of our Lord, and the believer's spiritual resurrection with Him, Rom vi. 4 ; the washing away of sin, see the same passage, also Acts ii. 38, and xxii. 16.

The other teaches—

1. The sufferings of Christ on the cross. This is my body which is broken for you, thus recalling to mind the passage in Isaiah liii. 5. So the wine poured out indicates the blood shed on the cross for us, and points to the truth, that without shedding of blood, there can be no remission of sin. Thus viewed it bears a close analogy to the Passover. That was instituted in memory of a great event in Jewish history, a great deliverance accomplished. As often as the children of Israel partook thereof, they were reminded of the destroying angel, of the blood-sprinkled door posts, of the wailing cry in Egypt, of the paschal lamb slain, roasted and eaten in hot haste, their loins girded, shoes on their feet, staves in their hands. These were facts, emblematic of God's mighty power, of their own helplessness, and of the wondrous deliverance effected.

The Lord's Supper teaches us, of our guilt and danger, our helplessness and ruin ; of God's infinite love ; of Christ's divine compassion ; of His awful sufferings, and of our deliverance from the thraldom of death and hell.

Not only so, there is also a subjective meaning attached to the observance of this rite. Take the 6th chapter of John's Gospel, and read ten verses from the 48th to the 58th. This was the hard saying which some of his disciples could not bear, and walked no more with him.

Food may be so prepared as to gratify the eye, but merely to gaze upon it, will do us no physical good. It must be taken into the mouth, eaten up and digested. If it be wholesome, it makes blood, and is distributed throughout the body, performing its functions. and quickening the whole man into active vigorous life. So the doctrines of the gospel, may be looked at as statements, and even pondered. but they do no good, unless they are taken into the under-tanding, the conscience, and the heart. Then they produce spiritual life.— Except ye eat the flesh of the Son of man, and drink His b ood ye have no life in you. The Redeemer nourishes our spiritual life as food nourishes the natural life, and we realize the force of the expression. " We are members of his body, of his flesh and of his bones." Conversion involves a personal reception of Christ for ourselves, into our hearts.

III. Let us consider in the third place, the class of persons entitled to partake of this rite.

1. It 's very evident that the careless, the worldly, and the profane, have no claim to be admitted to the privilege.

2. Neither, as we have already shewn, are we authorized to invite those who are seeking salvation, who have never wholly given themselves to Christ, and have no sense of pardon or acceptance.

3. Those who first partook were disciples of the Lord. " Drink ye all of it." Whom is he here address-ing ? Evidently those who professed to believe. Though there was a Judas among them, he avowed as much attachment to Christ, as the others. To whom did the Apostle, in the Epistle to the Corinthians, give directions about its due observance? " Unto the Church of God, which is at Corinth, to them that are sanctified in Christ Jesus, called to be saints."

4. It is evident from this that they were not only regenerate but baptized. The Apostle says again. When ye are come together in the Church. 1 Cor. xi. 18. See also John iv. 1, Acts ii. 41, 42. The Supper is then an ordinance of the church, to be held in the church and nowhere else. The church also, has authority to decide, who may and who may not partake, and the church alone.

In these views, we agree sub-tantially with our Presbyterian and Congregational brethren, though we differ from our Episcopalian and Wesleyan brethren on some points.

This statement will perhaps surprise some persons. We have been taunted so frequently with the exclusiveness of our close communion sentiments, as they are termed, that persons are very apt to suppose us bigotted in the extreme, when the reverse is the case. We set up no barriers which others do not set up. We are in fact less exclu-ive than some others. Were we disposed to retort, we might truly say, that they effectually exclude a large and ever increasing number of their brethren and sisters, from the Lord's table. They making that baptism which is nowhere commanded, and thus place the matter in such a light, as to make it impossible for us, without a manifest violation of our principles, to commune with them. Although there are open Communion Baptists, many in England, and a few on this continent, their position is anomalous, and the mode of argument, by which they attempt to justify that position, is such, that, if carried to its logical results, it would nullify the ordinance of baptism altogether.

IV. Finally. The question arises, What are the duties enjoined upon those who partake?

1. Self examination. But let a man examine himself, 1 Cor. xi. 28. There is danger, even of the christian eating and drinking unworthily. Many temporal judgements seem to have come upon the Church at Corinth, on this account. Many were weak and sickly among them, and many slept. Test your motives. Try your hearts. See whether you be sincere in your profession, stedfast in your attachment to Christ. If the result of such examination be unfavorable, let that drive you, not away from the table, but to confession and to prayer. If we confess our sins, God is faithful and just to forgive us our sins, and to cleanse us from all unrighteousness.

2. Again. If thou bringest thy gift to the altar, and there rememberest that thy brother hath aught against thee, go be reconciled to thy brother. Confess your faults against one another, one to another.

3. Remember Christ, especially in His own ordinances. Cultivate a spirit receptive of His teaching. Endeavour to apprehend that for which you also are apprehended of Christ.

Let your heart go out in love toward the body of Christ, and more especially to that church with which you are individually connected. Let your consecration of yourself, to your Saviour, be renewed as often as you meet Him at His table. Remember that you are not your own. As often as the emblems of His broken body, and shed blood, are received by you, let the language of the poet be yours:

> " Were the whole realm of nature mine—
> That were a present far too small;
> Love so amazing, so divine,
> Demands my life, my soul, my all."

If with these feelings, we, from time to time endeavour to meet our Lord, the formality otherwise inseparable from a statedly recurring observance, will disappear. It will be a source of never-failing delight. We ourselves quickened and renewed. will advance in the life of God, our usefulness will be increased, our sympathies drawn out. This largely experienced will make the church to be wonderously admired and multitudes will join themselves to us.

Appendix.

(A)

INFIRM MINISTERS' FUND *in acct. with* D. R. EATON, *Treasurer.*

1870.   DR.
July 4. To cash paid J. W. Barss, on account of Rev.
                              A. D. Thompson...................$20 00
Aug. 12.   "   "   Mrs. Walker, per Rev. Dr. Tupper. 10 00
1871.
June 1. To balance brought down to new account..........532 76
                                                          $562 76

1870.   CR.
June 1. By balance account rendered............$422 05
July 11. " Cash from John Steele, As. Treasurer. 55 17
Nov. 7. " Collection 1st. Cornwallis Church... .   6 91
 "   0. " Cash from LaHave Church...........   2 10
 "   9.   "   "   Bridgewater Church.......   3 90
Dec. 27.   "   "   Chester Church...........   5 33
1871.
June 1. " 1 year's Interest on the Jacob's Legacy. 40 06
 "   1. " Balance Interest to date............. 27 24
                                                     ——$562 76
1871.
June 1. By balance brought down................$532 76
                E. & O. E.
                        D. R. EATON, Treas. Infirm Ministers' Fund.
Cornwallis, June 24th, 1871.   Per C. F. E.

(B)
ON MISSIONS.

Your Committee beg to report that in their opinion no subject which invites the attention, sympathies and united efforts of this body, presents greater claims than th t of Missions. Viewed, either in its relation to the fulfilment of the glorious prediction which declares that the "kingdoms of this world shall become the kingdom of our Lord and of his Christ," or in connection with its practical bearing upon the prosperity of those engaged in the work, it reaches a sublimity unsurpassed by any other subject.

While the proclamation of the gospel and the emancipation of men from the corruptions of idolatry and the thraldom of sin in all its forms are the exalted aims of all true missionary enterprise, it is a well attested fact that the work itself where vigorously pursued in the spirit of the Master has a tendency to quicken the pulse of spiritual life, and becomes an element of vitality and power, as well as a source of unmingled enjoyment.

The Home and Foreign Missions, in the judgment of your committee, are so intimately connected and of such vital importance that it becomes difficult to decide which presents the stronger claims. It is evident from our Lord's teaching together with the great Commission that the "field is the world," and every believer in Christ is called upon to be a labourer in this great field. When the great missionary enterprise was launched forth upon the world, Jerusalem was its centre of operations its theater of action was limited only by the boundaries of the entire world.

Your Committee are conscious that the efforts of our denomination in this department are not at all in proportion to our means, and the necessity of the demands of a sin-suffering world, yet it is gratifying to learn that something is being done.

In the Foreign Department although the Baptists of these provinces have not what is termed an Independent mission, yet there are abundant channels through which their benevolence may flow and accomplish the end so ardently desired, the salvation of the heathen. Intelligence from time to time of the marked success of Native preachers, supported by our churches, sabbath schools, and by individuals is truly encouraging, and evidently show that our efforts are stamped with the seal of Divine approval. The departure of our beloved sister, Miss Norris, during the past year, and her safe arrival on the field of her future labors awaken feelings of devout gratitude to God, and the fact that there are young men among us whose hearts are burning with an unquenchable desire to tell the story of the cross to the benighted, and are diligently preparing for that work, encourage the belief that at no distant day the Baptists of these provinces will have a strong and efficient force, successfully prosecuting this glorious work.

The praiseworthy efforts of our sisters in forming Woman's Aid Societies to supply means for carrying on the work, cannot be too highly commended, and your Committee strongly recommend the formation of similar societies in all our churches, with the hope that our brethren will be stimulated by their noble example to greater exertions in the work of Missions.

In the Home department great good has been accomplished. Weak churches have been confirmed, and souls have been converted as the report of the Home Mission Society testifies; and although the machinery by which the work is carried on is by no means perfect. or as efficient as it ought to be, yet in view of past success and present prospects we have reason to thank God and take courage.

The French Missionary Bro. Normanday is still pursuing his work, with what success we are not able to say not being in possession of any direct information. We believe, however, that God is in the work.

In conclusion your commmittee would commend the interests of missions generally to the fervant prayers of all God's people.

"Thy Kingdom come," understood-comprehended and uttered in view of the tremendous responsibilities resting upon us as stewards of the manifold grace of God as well as His providential bestowments, will lead us to a more entire consecration of ourselves and our possessions to Him who has bought us with a price and has commanded us to glorify God in our bodies and spirits which are God's.

Respectfully submitted,
I. J. SKINNER, *Chairman*.

(C)

ON EDUCATION.

The Committee rejoice that they live in a country where education is valued and amply provided for, and where the poorest may obtain knowledge. The School-law of this Province, judiciously and vigorously administered, cannot but prove a blessing of priceless worth.

In the higher branches of education facilities are now fully furnished. Our Denomination, has largely shared in the honour of making provision for the thorough training of the young men of the Province, and has been rewarded with encouraging success. There are many persons, occupying positions of trust, responsibility, and usefulness, and standing in the first ranks of their respective professions, whose powers were developed and disciplined in our Institutions. Horton Academy and Acadia College have been for many years great blessings, not only to the Baptists, but also to Nova Scotia at large. Our co-religionists acknowledge the truth of this statement, while we ourselves freely admit the merits of other Institutions, which have deserved well of their country.

The College, we are happy to report, continues to pursue a prosperous career, under the presidency of Dr. Sawyer. Twelve students graduated at the last Anniversary, and it is expected that a large Class will matriculate at the commencement of the next Collegiate year.

Arrangements are now made by which ministerial students, spending a fifth year in College, that is, remaining another year after graduation, wholly occupied in Theological pursuits, will be far better prepared for the work to which

2

they have devoted themselves than if they were to be transferred at once from literary engagements to pulpit and pastoral labours. These arrangements, however, will ere long require to be supplemented by an increase of the professorial staff. There will then be no necessity for our candidates for the ministry to go out of the country in order to pursue their professional studies, thus exposing themselves to the temptation to settle for life on a foreign soil, and depriving their native land of the benefits that might accrue from the employment of their talents there. It may surely be expected that Baptist Licentiates will be prompt to avail themselves of the advantages now offered them. The progress of society renders it imperative on those who propose to become religious instructors to "seek and intermeddle with all wisdom."

The Committee are assured that the Governors are desirous of the further improvement of the College in all respects. They would willingly furnish more ample accomodation to the students, on the College premises. The library greatly needs an enlarged supply of books in the various branches of literature, as well as in Theology and Ecclesiastical History, and a new building is urgently required for the use of the Library and Museum. A considerable sum of money ought to be expended in putting the college buildings into a state of respectable repair. But the want of means stands in the way of the accomplishment of these purposes. Wealthy Baptists might render immense service to Denominational interests by devoting a few thousands to their advancement.

The Committee desire to commend the Academy to the especial regard of the denomination. It is in successful operation, and the number of students is increasing. It is the only Institution which acts as a feeder to the College by supplying the necessary prepation for College studies, under the supervision and control of the Governors. Young men who propose to take a College course should be earnestly recommended to en ter the Academy, and to remain there a sufficiently long time to secure adequate fitness for the higher exercises in which they are to be engaged..

A superficial preparation is much to be deprecated. It is far better for the student to spend two or more years in the Academy than to hasten his entry into the College before the proper time.

It is much to be lamented that in addition to the objects referred to above there is as yet but little prospect of the erection of a Female Seminary, or of a building for the joint use of males and females, for educational purposes. But why cannot this most desirable object be effected? What hinders the Baptists of Nova Scotia from raising a fund of twenty thousand dollars, and making immediate provision for the

liberal education of their daughters as well as their sons?
The mothers demand it of us. The country demands it.
The Church demands it. In the name of all—invoking the
blessing of God—"let us arise and build."

Respectfully submitted,
J. M. Cramp, *Chairman.*

(D)
ON OBITUARIES.

Your Committee find that one brother in the ministry and
a number of esteemed brethren in the churches have been
removed by death during the past year:

Rev. Nelson Baker departed this life, July 11th, 1870,
after a few days of intense suffering which he bore with submission to the divine will. This brother had for a few years been
residing in the neighborhood of Halifax where he had been
enabled to provide for the wants of a large family. After he
had made his family comfortable, he engaged anew in the
work of the ministry. A revival attended his labours in
Tancook, and it was on his return to this place for the purpose
of preaching the gospel, that he was seized with his last
sickness. Our brother was an earnest preacher, and a strong
advocate of ministerial education. He availed himself of
every opportunity to qualify himself in this respect for the
great work in which he was engaged. Our brother leaves a
widow and a large family of children to mourn their loss.
May the rich blessing of the God of the widow and fatherless
be abundantly bestowed upon the mourners.

James Walton Nutting, D. C. L. deacon of Granville
Street Church, fell asleep in Jesus on the 7th of July 1870,
in the 84th year of his age. Our departed brother was a
member of the first class that graduated at King's College,
Windsor. He subsequently studied law, and was admitted
to the Nova Scotia Bar in 1810; and after entering upon
active life in the legal profession he was appointed Prothonotary of the Supreme Court and Clerk of the Crown in
Halifax, which offices he held till the close of life. He was a
learned man,—and a good man. He lived in the highest
esteem of all who knew him, and his memory is cherished in
the warmest affection by all his brethren in Christ! He
helped to found our Institutions of learning and never
withdrew his sympathies from them. He rendered valuable
service to the cause of Christ, and the Baptist denomination,
by assisting to start the *Christian Messenger*—the first
weekly religious newspaper in these provinces,—and con-

tinued to contribute, more or less, to its pages up to within a few weeks of his death.

He had the rare power of making all men his friends, and among all who knew him at his death not an enemy could be found.

God has also taken from among us Deacons Theodorus Kinsman, (of the 3rd Cornwallis Church); J. P. Graves, (of the Upper Aylesford Church); Wm. Skinner, (of the 2nd Cornwallis Church); and brethren Wm. Shaw of Falmouth, and Mabew Beckwith of Canard.

We cannot make extended notice of all these excellent brethren separately, but of all we feel glad to say, that they were good men, and full of faith. Each has left to the world, a pleasing tribute to the power and beauty of the gospel of Christ.

Bro. Mahew Beckwith, was for many years a member of the 1st Cornwallis Church and to the very last manifested much interest in all the enterprises of the denomination. His attendance upon the public services of the Church was very punctual, and his death has made a painful blank in the congregation among whom he worshipped. He was at the time of his death a member of the Board of Governors of Acadia College, and in sympathy and fellowship with all his brethren.

Bro. William Shaw of Falmouth, was well and long known by all the ministers of our Association and esteemed by them for his amiability, and generous hospitality. His house had been a home for good men for many years, and he himself a lover of such. He professed faith in Christ quite late in life, but for years had possessed the adornment of a meek and quiet spirit.

The death of Bro. J. P. Graves was sudden and unexpected. He seemed cut down in the midst of usefulness and promise. The master had need of him, and he was ready to depart.

Bro. Kinsman died an old man, full of days, amiable, discreet and eminently pious.

Deacon Wm. Skinner was one of the first members of the 2nd Cornwallis Church. He was known among his brethren for the clearness and firmness with which he held the doctrines of the gospel. He was faithful unto death.

S. B. Kempton, *Chairman.*

(E)
ON BENEVOLENT OBJECTS.

Your Committee beg leave to report:—

That they are apprehensive that the systematic and continued efforts recommended last year by the Committee on Benevolent Objects have not been made by the churches of this Association. Had it been so, the increase in the funds would have been greater than appears from the letters of the Churches. Your Committee would endorse the sentiments of the report of last year, and urge them upon the attention of the Association. In addition to systematic and sustained efforts, indispensable to success in raising funds for denominational objects, there are, in the opinion of your Committee, two or three considerations which merit the attention of this Association. In the earlier days of our denominational history, not a tithe of the wealth, possessed by the Baptists now, was then in their hands. A high standard of benevolence was impossible at the beginning. This measure of liberality has been too generally retained in the memories of the older and too generally adopted by the younger members of our denomination. Had we not increased in numbers our increase of wealth would be of no service. The increase in our contributions is not in proportion to our increase in both wealth and numbers, but numbers alone. Scholarships of four hundred dollars ought now to be four thousand dollars. The few shillings to missions by individuals ought now to be as many pounds. The old standards are a delusion and a snare. It is a time for taking down these old ones, and erecting new and higher ones. The giving should not be according to the measure in the past, but according to the means of the present. Advantage also ought to be taken of the special interest shown by individuals in particular objects. Let those enthusiastic for education be encouraged to put down their hundreds and thousands to the Endowment Fund of the College to the building of a new Academy and Seminary for young ladies, or for a fund to support young men studying for the ministry, as the case may be. A special sympathy will thus be engendered for particular objects and larger helping and fostering care extended to them. The evidence of this appears in the contributions which are coming almost spontaneously from all parts of the province for the support of native preachers in the East. This tendency should not be repressed. When all our denominational objects are presented every one in whose heart there is a benevolent impulse, and every one capable of such a feeling will be drawn toward some object. In this way the strongest sympathies will be cultivated, and the greatest amount of means raised.

E. M. SAUNDERS, *Chairman.*

Amounts forwarded by the Churches to the Association, for Benevolent Objects, June, 1871.

CHURCHES.	Home Missions.	Foreign Missions.	French Mission.	Ministerial Education.	Acadia College.	Infirm Ministers.	TOTAL.
Aylesford Upper........	$0 00	$8 00	$8 00	$	$15 00	$3 00	$43 00
Bridgewater............	12 50	15 25	5 00	4 25		5 00	42 00
Burton................	4 25						4 25
Chester...............	24 30	33 89	.....	3 62	10 80	4 75	77 16
Chelsea...............	5 00	5 00	5 00	4 31	5 00	5 00	29 31
Cornwallis 1st.........	21 47	43 56	10 75	8 87	15 00	9 37	109 03
Cornwallis 2nd.........	20 25	19 00	7 50	1 25	12 00	5 00	65 00
Cornwallis 3rd.........	13 62	3 09	1 37	.....	10 37	1 62	30 09
Cornwallis 5th.........	6 40	8 25	.....	1 00	7 50	91	24 06
Cornwallis 6th.........	4 27	11 25	2 50	25	10 62	1 63	30 53
Fall River............	3 00						3 00
Falmouth..............	8 00	8 00	4 00	2 12	.....	.....	22 12
Greenfield............	.....	10 50					10 50
Halifax 2nd...........	40 00	40 00	16 00	.....	40 00	12 00	148 00
Hammonds Plains.......	10 00	7 40					17 40
Hammonds Plains 2nd...	.....	.....	.....	.....	2 00		2 00
Hantsport............	14 00	.....	4 00	3 00	9 92	3 40	34 32
Horton 1st............	.....	53 00	.....	11 65	.....	.....	64 65
Horton 2nd...........	8 87	5 20	1 00	62	1 35	3 20	20 25
Horton 3rd...........	9 00	8 00	4 00	.....	.....	2 00	23 00
Indian Harbor........	6 00	6 00	2 50				14 50
Jeddore..............	4 00	2 50					6 50
Kempt...............	4 32	11 30	1 56	.....	5 37	.....	22 56
LaHave..............	3 00	3 00	.....	1 50	4 00	1 50	13 00
Lunenburg...........	12 00	4 00	2 00	2 00	15 00	4 00	30 00
Musquodoboit........	3 00	1 00					4 00
Maitland............	6 00	1 00	.....	.....	3 00		10 00
New Germany........	3 95	28 17	1 07	.....	7 62	.....	41 02
Newport East........	2 00	4 00	1 12	.....	8 00	.....	15 12
New Ross............	8 00	2 00					10 00
New Cornwall........	5 00	5 00	2 00	1 70	.....	.....	13 70
Preston 1st..........	3 50						3 50
Preston 2nd..........	2 00						2 00
Rawdon.............	4 80	5 00	2 00	1 75	3 25	3 29	20 00
Sackville...........	22 75	4 25	1 30	.....	8 16	4 15	40 61
St Margarets Bay.....	9 75	7 12	3 87	62	.....	50	21 87
Tancook.............	.....	.....	.....	.....	4 00	.....	4 00
Windsor.............	100 00	100 00	5 00	.....	40 00	5 00	250 00
Sab. Coll. of Cornwallis 1st.	3 50						3 50
Cornwallis 5th........	27 17						27 17
Cornwallis 6th........	6 27						6 25
Hon. E. Churchell.....	50 00	50 00					100 00
Miss Lockwood Dimock...	1 50						1 50
	502 54	513 74	92 36	48 54	237 67	75 24	$1470 10
Expenses..............	40 12	.....	7 44	3 87	.....	6 07	57 50
	462 42	513 74	84 92	44 67	237 67	69 17	$1412 60

WILLIAM C. BILL,   } Treasurers.
EDWIN RAND,

Baptist Association, Pereaux, Cornwallis, }
    June 27th, 1871.

Amounts reported in the Letters to have been set apart by the Churches, for the objects specified below, in addition to the moneys forwarded to the Treasurer of the Association

NAME OF CHURCH. 1	Missions. 2	Education. 3	Infirm Ministers. 4	Pastor's Salary. 5	Current Expenses. 6	Meeting House. 7	Parsonage. 8	Church Poor. 9	Other Purposes. 10	Total. 11
Bridgewater	$60 40	$10 00		$350 00	$52 52		$28 37		$115 00	$616 30
Canning	17 22	10 67	$1 63	200 00	40 00				58 52	328 39
Chester			5 53						7 50	13 03
Cornwallis 1st., Canard	107 67	40 00	10 90	600 00	90 00	$900 00			214 73	962 62
Cornwallis 2nd., Berwick	70 32			500 00	30 00				150 00	1350 32
Cornwallis 3rd., Billtown	144 90			400 00	24 00					663 00
Cornwallis 5th., Pereaux	24 81			200 00	36 00					449 98
Hantsport			6 00	550 00		147 17		$65 00	73 00	646 00
Horton 1st., Wolfville	200 00	111 00		200 00					25 00	380 00
Horton 2nd., Gaspereaux	32 99	9 05							150 00	382 05
Jeddore	4 00	6 00							6 00	370 00
LaHave	4 00			70 00	290 00	350 00			2 10	212 10
Lunenburg, North West						136 00			40 00	249 00
New Germany	23 00			300 00	16 00				8 00	359 00
Rawdon	18 00			163 00	20 00					201 02
Windsor	250 00	280 00	5 00	500 00	200 00	500 00	60 00	25 00	300 00	2130 60
	$1028 56	$408 93	$29 00	$4226 00	$706 52	$1733 17	$88 37	$90 00	$1221 67	$9465 00

Statistics of the Churches in the N. S. Central Association, 1871.

NAME OF CHURCH.	Date of Organization.	PASTOR'S NAME.	Year of Settlement.	CLERK AND POST OFFICE ADDRESS.	By Baptism.	By Letter, &c.	Restored.	Dismissed.	Excluded.	Died.	Present Membership.
1 Aylesford, Upper	1846	Rev. J. L. Read		Whitman Morton	4	6		1		2	191
2 Bridgewater	1846	Rev. S. March		W. A. C. Randall, M. D.	7	10		2		2	133
3 Burton											31
4 Canning	1870	Rev. D. Freeman	1861	James S. Witter, Canning	2				1		37
5 Chelsea				Andrew Jeans							97
6 Chester			1861	John A. Church	5			3	3	1	263
7 Cornwallis 1st, Canard	1811	Rev. I. J. Skinner	1868	Otis Eaton, Upper Canard	11	5		19		2	374
8 Cornwallis 2nd, Berwick	1811	Rev. S. B. Kempton	1868	T. H. Parker, Berwick	4	6		2	1	5	442
9 Cornwallis 3rd, Billtown	1875	Rev. J. F. Kempton	1870	Mesaiah Kinsman, Billtown	32	11		5		3	401
10 Cornwallis 4th, Long Point											117
11 Cornwallis 5th, Pereaux	1802	Rev. D. Freeman	1801	D. H. Newcomb, Lower Pereaux	19	4	2	1		2	101
12 Dartmouth		Rev. A. S. Hunt		J. W. Johnston, Jr.	1	1		1		2	44
13 Falmouth	1843	Rev. Joseph Murr...	1870	A. Shaw, Falmouth	15	2		2	2	3	93
14 Fall River											30
15 Halifax 1st, Granville St.	1827	Rev. E. M. Saun...	1867	H. Eaton, Halifax	8	13		5	1	1	107
16 Halifax 2nd, North	1845	Rev. J. E. Goucher		A. W. Clark, No. 3 Munford Terrace, Halifax	12	22		1	2	6	390
17 Hammond's Plains 1st	1842			Amos Bezanson, A...	10			4	1		47
18 Hammond's Plains 2nd				No Statistics							63
19 Hantsport		Rev. J. Murray	1870	W. E. West	16	11	1	1		5	278

	Minister		Minister						Total
20 Horton 1st, Wolfville	1789	Rev. S. W. DeBlois	1856	D. F. Higgins	45	12			9	287
21 Horton 2nd, Gaspereaux	1841		1871	T. E. Martin	32	1		1	2	288
22 Horton 3rd, New Minas			1868	Calvin Bishop	4					180
23 Indian Harbor	1843	Rev. James Parker	1868	Elias Covey						83
24 Jeddore		Rev. T. C. Delong		Enos Baker	6	1		1	6	91
25 Kempt		Rev. J. Meadows	1906	Joseph D. Masters	1				3	139
26 LaHave		Rev. Geo. Weathers	1860	John Lantz, Pleasantville					5	33
27 Lunenburg	1809	Rev. S. March		George A. Parker					1	127
28 Maitland				David L. McCurdy	4					21
29 Musquodoboit	1854	Rev. R. R. Philp		Francis Layton	2	3			1	16
30 New Cornwall			1871	John Spidle	18	1		3		49
31 New Germany	1856	Rev. W. E. Hall	1864	A. E. Durland	6	1				175
32 Newport East	1842	Rev. W. E. Hall		Sterns Dimock				4	3	78
33 Newport West	1850	Rew. J. Bancroft		Joseph Walley				3	1	120
34 New Ross				Joseph Lantz				1	2	45
35 Preston 1st, (No Statistics.										42
36 Preston 2nd,										12
37										
38 Rawdon	1823			John McLearn		3		2		132
40 Sackville	1825			F. Webber	4				6	20
41 St. Margaret's Bay	1853	Rev. T. C. Delong		Benjamin I. Hubley				4	4	100
42 Tancook				Albert Pearl				7	2	111
43 Walton										16
44 Waterville										12
45 Windsor	1819	Rev. D. M. Welton			18	2			6	191
46 Windsor Plains		James Johnson	1857	Thomas I. L. Bennet	2				3	19
					294	133	14	94	39 88	5712

*No letter for one year. †No letter for three years. ‡No letter for four years.

*No letter for four years, but retained on Minutes by request.

Statistics of Sabbath Schools in the Central Baptist Association, June, 1871.

SCHOOLS.	SUPERINTENDENT.	SCHOLARS. Male	Female	Total	Ave'ge attendance.	TEACHERS. Male	Female	Total	No. in Bible Class.	Members of Church in B. C. and S. S.	Vols. in Library.	Expended during the year.
Aylesford, Upper*	W. J. Gates	38	31	67	54	4	3	7		7	270	$30 00
Bridgewater*	James Falt	48	40	88	35	4	4	8	12	10	150	
Do. Pleasantville	Mrs. James Johnson	15	17	32	36	5		5		1		
Do. CreneTown	Rev. S. March	10	10	20	20		4	4		7		
Do. Lakerville	do. do.									6		
Do. Lapland									34			
Canning	J. S. Witter	40	50	90	70	4	3	11	25	20	250	38 86
Chelsea	William Faulkner	17	23	40	30	4	3	6	20	7	100	7 67
Chester Town	Daniel Exter	14	17	31	45	4	4	8	10	11	80	
Do. Core*	Edw. Heckman	35	16	37	33	3	3	8				
Do. Basin*	A. Anderson	27	28	55	50	4	4	8	30	12	200	
Do. Windsor Road		10	10	20	20							
Cornwallis 1st., Canard*	Joseph Webber	51	50	101	82	5	6	11	42	6	80	
Do. Lower Canard*	J. E. Lockwood	45	60	105	89	3	9	12	20	12	200	63 00
Do. Port Williams*	D. R. Eaton	43	63	100	65	3	4	9	11	3	200	
Cornwallis 2nd*	T. H. Borden	90	100	180	140	14	9	23	75	45	240	
Cornwallis 3rd., Billtown‡	A. F. Chipman	40	45	85	75	5	6	11	8		150	14 00
Cornwallis 5th., Pereaux*	Melatiah Kinsman	43	41	74	30	6	5	11	30	24	250	12 00
Do. Scot's Bay Road	E. C. West											
Dartmouth*	D. H. Newcomb			30	30	4						
Falmouth 1st.	B. Pitts	25	45	30	30	2	2	4		13		17 00
Do. 2nd, Village	A. Shaw	45	27	68	60	4	5	9			150	10 00
Halifax 1st., Granville Street‡	E. Christopher	80	90	170	94	9	11	20	22	22	600	125 74
	F. H. Rand											

Location	Name												
Hantsport	A. W. Clark												$1 34
Hantsport, Brooklyn	Amos Margeson												5 40
Horton 1st, Wolfville	Rev. ... Murray												120 00
Do. 2nd, Gaspereaux	Geo. N. Ballentine												10 50
Do. Do. Greenfield	J. W. Allen												
Do. Do. Black River	Kinson Gould												
Indian Harbor	Jno. Pick. Senr.												
Jeddore West	George Richardson												
Jeddore East	Jeremiah Harpell												
Kempt, (2 schools)	Enos Baker												
LaHave	Levi Minard & Jas. Greeno.												
Lunenburg, Mahone Bay	Jonas B. Parker.												90 00
Lunenburg, North West	Joseph Hamm.												4 00
Maitland	Obediah Parker.												
New Cornwall	Rev. R. R. Philp.												8 00
New Germany*	Caleb Soldie.												
Do. Foster Settlement*	Geo. S. Bares.												
Do. Branch*	Edw. Kaulback.												
Rawdon, South*	Wm. Wagner.												
Do. Hilldale*	G. J. Creed.												
Do. Mount Uniacke*	James Canavan.												
St. Margaret's Bay	E. Brymer.												
Tancook	Alvan Hubley.												
Windsor	Alfred Baker.												
Horton 3rd, New Minas*	Rev. D. M. Welton.												200 00
Do. New Canaan	Edw. L. Bishop.												
	do. do.												
													$885 71

* The Statistics of these Schools given as last year.
† This School raised $100 to support a Bible Woman in Burmah.
‡ There are four other Schools in connection with this church, no Statistics given.
§ This School raised in addition the sum of $55.32 for Foreign Missions.
‖ This School raised $75 in addition for a Native Teacher in Burmah.

NAMES.	Present Residence.	Date of Ordination.	Place of Ordination.
Rev. Balcom, James E...	Hantsport, N.S.	March 26, 1853	Long Island.
" Bancroft, Jeremiah,	Walton........	March 8, 1849	Rawdon.
" Cramp, J. M., D. D.	Wolfville	May 7, 1818	London, G. B.
" Crawley, E. A., D.D.	Wolfville	May 28, 1830	Providence, R. I.
" Chase, John........	Wolfville	—, 1835	Billtown.
" Clay, Edwin. M. D..	Halifax........		
" DeBlois, S. W., A.M.	Wolfville	Feb. 26, 1854	Chester.
" Freeman, D., A. M.	Canning.	Aug. —, 1855	Halifax.
" Goucher, J. E........	Halifax........	Oct. 5, 1859	Gagetown, N. B.
" Hall. W. E.........	New Germany.	Sept. 23, 1864	New Germany.
" Higgins, T. A., A.M.	Wolfville	Aug. 30, 1857	Liverpool.
" Hunt, A. S., A. M.	Dartmouth	Nov. 10, 1844	Dartmouth.
" Kempton, J. F., A.B.	Billtown	June 5, 1864	Mira, C. B.
" Kempton, S.B., A.M.	Canard	Sept. 16, 1863	New Minas.
" March, Stephen.....	Bridgewater	July 5, 1856	St. Francis, N. B.
" Meadows, James...	Jeddore........	Feb. 26, 1868	Jeddore.
" Miller, John.........	Halifax.......		
" Murray, Jos. A. B...	Hantsport......	Nov. —, 1865	Guysborough.
" Newcomb, James...	Wolfville		Hillsborough, N. B.
" Parker, James......	New Minas	May 10, 1842	Upper Wilmot.
" Pineo, D............	Long Point	Dec. 24, 1844	Greenwich.
" Rand, S. T.........	Hantsport	Oct. 7, 1834	Cornwallis.
" Read, E. O.........	Berwick	Jan. 8, 1858	Gaspereaux.
" Read, J. L.........	Up. Aylesford..	June 30, 1858	Hopewell, N. B.
" Saunders, E.M., A.M.	Halifax......	Dec. 15, 1856	West Cornwallis.
" Sawyer, A. W. D. D.	Wolfville	1853	Lawrence, Mass. U.S.
" Shaw, D. G........	Falmouth.....	Jan. 24, 1860	Falmouth.
" Shields, P. A.......	Mahone Bay ...	July 18, 1852	Hantsport.
" Skinner, I. J., A. B..	Chester........	Sept. 19, 1858	Port Medway.
" Stevens, James.....	Gaspereaux. ..	Aug. 4, 1830	Horton.
" Vaughan, B.........	Kempt........	May 4, 1842	Wolfville.
" Weathers, George..	Kempt.......	May 12, 1864	Newport.
" Welton, D. M., A.M.	Windsor	Sept. 2, 1857	Windsor.

LICENTIATES.

Charles Norwood, 2nd. Cornwallis.
Obadiah Parker, Lunenburg.
Isaac Skinner, 2nd. Cornwallis.
John Wallace, 1st. Cornwallis.
Edw. Whitman, Halifax, 2nd.
Jacob Allen, (colored), New Guysborough road.
George Carvery, (colored), Preston 2nd.

CONSTITUTION

OF THE

Central Baptist Association of N. J.

ARTICLE 1st.—This Association shall consist of Delegates representing the Churches of which it is composed, each of whom shall be a member of one of those Churches, together with Delegates from Corresponding Associations, not exceeding five from any one Association, and such other brethren present as the Association may see fit to invite to sit in Council.

ART. 2nd.—The Association shall meet at such time and place as may be agreed upon by the body.

ART. 3rd.—Each Church shall have the privilege of sending one Delegate or more, but no Church shall be entitled to send more than five in addition to their Pastor.

ART. 4th.—At each meeting of the Association the Moderator of the preceding year shall preside till his successor is chosen. The choice of Moderator shall take place by ballot, as soon as a list of Delegates has been prepared, as hereinafter provided. No brother shall be chosen Moderator two years in succession. It shall be the duty of the Moderator to preside in all the transactions, maintain due order, and nominate Committees, unless otherwise ordered by the Association. A Secretary shall be chosen, whose duty it shall be to record the transactions of the Association, and to furnish a correct copy of the same for the press; he is also to remain in office till his successor is chosen.

ART. 5th.—It shall be the duty of each Church to send by his messengers a letter to the Association giving an account of its state, particularly of the additions and diminutions within the last year, and generally of whatsoever relates to its peace and prosperity.

ART. 6th.—At each Annual Meeting the letters from the Churches shall be first handed in, from which the Secretary shall immediately make out a list of Delegates. The election of Moderator and Secretary shall then take place, after which the letters shall be read. Committees nominated by the Moderator shall not consist of more than five brethren, of whom three shall constitute a quorum. When large Committees are judged desirable they shall be appointed by the Association, and two-thirds of the members appointed shall be competent to act.

ART. 7th.—When any Church shall desire admittance into this body, application must be made by letter, and satisfactory evidence furnished of its faith and order; this being done, and a vote of acceptance taken, the Moderator shall, in the behalf of the Association, give to one of its messengers present the right-hand of fellowship.

ART. 8th.—When any Church shall neglect to make communication for three years successively it shall be considered as having withdrawn from us, and shall be dropped from the Minutes, unless two or more members shall request its continuance and shall engage to enquire into its standing, and report at the next meeting of the Association

Art. 9th.—Although as an Association all power over the Churches is disclaimed, so far as respects any interference with their independence and discipline ; yet it is deemed a privilege belonging to the Association to judge for itself of the propriety of receiving or retaining any Church in its connexion.

Art. 10th.—The religious sentiments of this body are those expressed in the " Articles of the Faith and Practice of the Baptist Churches in Nova Scotia."

Art. 11th.—That the Moderator be authorized at any time during the year, to call a special meeting of the Association. in pursuance of a requisition signed by ten members thereof.

Art. 12.—Alterations and amendments may be made to this Constitution by a vote of two-thirds of the members present at any of its regular meetings.

RULES OF ORDER.

Rule 1st.—At every sitting, business shall be opened and closed with prayer ; and immediately after the opening, the Minutes of the preceding meeting shall be read and corrected.

Rule 2nd.—No member of the Association shall leave the Session before the business is concluded, without permission of the Association.

Rule 3rd.—No subject shall be discussed without a motion first made and seconded.

Rule 4th.—No person shall speak oftener than twice on the same subject, unless by permission of the body.

Rule 5th.—Brethren invited to a seat with us may speak on all subjects under consideration, but vote on none.

Rule 6th.—All resolutions shall be presented in writing.

Rule 7th.—Motions made and lost shall not be recorded on the Minutes, except so ordered at the time.

Rule 8th.—These rules shall be distinctly read from the Chair at the opening of the Session.

FOURTEENTH ANNIVERSARY

OF THE

N. S. Home Missionary Society,

The Fourteenth Anniversary of the Nova Scotia Baptist Home Missionary Society, was held at Percaux, Cornwallis, June 16th, at 2½, P. M.

The President—Bro S. Selden in the chair.

The Annual Report of the Board was read by the Secretary, adopted, and ordered to be printed and circulated under the direction of the Board.

Deeply interesting addresses were delivered by Revs. Jas. Parker, T. C. Delong, Jas. Meadows, E. M. Saunders, R. R. Philp. Judge McCully, and Bro. Francis Webber.

The Treasurer's report was read and adopted.

The Secretary read a letter from Hon. Dr. Parker tendering his resignation of the office of Treasurer in consequence of his intended absence from the Province for some time.

Whereupon Judge McCully was appointed Treasurer in place of Hon. Dr. Parker whose resignation was accepted.

The following Officers and Board of Managers were appointed for the ensuing year.

Officers of the Society.

S. Selden, *President.*

John W. Barss, ⎱ *Vice President.*
John King, ⎰

Judge McCully, *Treasurer.*

R. N. Beckwith, *Secretary.*

John Steele, *Auditor.*

BOARD OF MANAGERS.

Rev. J. M. Cramp, D. D.	Bro. H. R. Cunningham,
" Edwin Clay, M. D.	" A. Clarke,
" S. W. DeBlois,	" Wm. Cummings,
" D. W. C. Dimock,	" Wm. Faulkner,
" J. E. Goucher,	" Edwin D. King,
" A. S. Hunt,	" H. N. Paint,
" G. F. Miles,	" J. F. L. Parsons,
" James Parker,	" L. S. Payzant,
" E. M. Saunders,	" T. H. Rand,
" D. A. Steele,	" Alex. Robinson,
" D. M. Welton,	" Francis Webber,

Bro. David Thompson.

Adjourned to meet with the Eastern Association in 1872.

R. N. BECKWITH, *Sec'y.*

FOURTEENTH ANNUAL REPORT.

The Board of Managers in presenting their report beg to state that fourteen Missionaries have been sent out under their direction during the year. *Five* of these have been laboring on the Island of Cape Breton, *two* in the Counties of Guysborough and Antigonishe, *one* in Colchester, *two* in Cumberland, Two in Hants, *one* in Kings, and *two* in Lunenburg.

Revs. Wm. McPhee and E. C. Spinney, have been in the service of the Board on the Islands of Cape Breton during the entire year.

Revs. E. B. Corey in Cumberland, and R. R. Philip in Hants, have each an appointment for twelve months, partially fulfilled. The other appointments made ranging from *five* to *ten* weeks each.

The whole number of weeks services is 225½ equivalent to *one* Missionary for about 4½ years ; Sermons preached 754 Prayer and Conference Meetings held 486 ; Family Visits 2110 ; Baptisms 73 ; Pages of Tracts distributed 10965 ; miles travelled 8469. £850,54½ has been collected by the Missionaries.

The Treasurer has received $250 more than was paid in last year. Thus in nearly every particular an improvement upon the preceeding year is manifest.

The success which has attended this department of Christian work during the year now closed, should be an incentive to increased activity, and zealous labour, in a cause which has been so evidently marked with Divine approval.

The work of Missions, or making known the truth as it is in Jesus, is an important part of the responsibility of the Churches of Christ.

The Redeemer when on earth bade his disciples " go into all the world and preach the Gospel to every creature" yet particularly required that they should " begin at Jerusalem" by which we may justly infer that the field embraced within the bounds of our Associations has a strong claim upon our attention, labor and sacrifice.

If we loved Christ with an affection corresponding to his love for us, we should feel that no sacrifice was too great for his honor, or if we cherished in our hearts anything like that love for perishing sinners, that brought him from heaven to earth, to seek and save that which was lost—how earnest how devoted, how ready should we be to lay our all at the

Saviour's feet, to be employed for His honour, and the eternal salvation of ruined men.

Much remains to be done; the fruit of faithful labor put forth in the past is yet to be gathered in, and it is our duty to continue sowing the seed, knowing that in due time an abundant harvest will be reaped.

Brethren—Let us awake to our responsibilities and enter upon the work of Home Evangelization with renewed zeal and strong confidence in Him who came to seek and save the perishing, let our interest in the cause of Christ become so intense, so earnest that we shall not rest satisfied until the multitudes within our bounds shall know the truths we believe, the ordinances we observe, and the reasons upon which our faith and pratice is founded.

GROSS RECEIPTS AND EXPENDITURES.

RECEIPTS.

Balance in Treasurer's hand June 1st, 1870.............		$211 94
Received during the year......................$937 49		
" Half-years Interest on Debentures.....	80 00	
		$967 49
Collected by the Missionaries.........................		850 04½
		$2029 47½

EXPENDITURE.

Collected and Retained by Missionaries.........$850 04½				
Disbursed by Treasurer for Travelling expenses	71 49			
" " Missionary labor.....	598 08½			
" " S. Selden, Reports, &c.	55 00			
" " Secretary for services.	75 00			
" " Stationery, Postage, &c.	5 40			
Balance in hand...........................	374 25½			
				$2029 47½

Liabilities of the Board for labor partially preformed about $600.

CAPE BRETON.

Rev. Wm. McPhee has continued to labor in the service of the Board during the year.

Preached 196 sermons attended 83 Prayer and Conference meetings, made 532 Family Visits, Baptized 8, collected £82.27½.

Extracts from letters received.

June 7th.—" This certainly is a time to strike for Cape Breton, a time to go forward and possess the land. May the Lord grant his people an aggressive, a missionary spirit. From Arichat to Cape North, the field is wide open for Baptist Missionaries. Baptist sympathy and sentiments are growing, for the people begin to read God's Word.

September 13th.—" Lord's day before last I baptized an

aged person at St. Anns. It was a special season, the Lord by His Spirit was indeed present. There were, probably, one thousand people sitting on the banks of the River, many of whom came to mock, but throughout the whole assemblage, solemn attention was paid, while I preached from the commission as recorded in the gospel by Matthew. The Lord grant to hasten the day of general awakening among the people.

April 4th, 1871.—Since writing to you last, I baptized one at Baddeck River. He was an aged man and his conversion was very remarkable. He could not read and consequently was dependant upon the few passages of God's word, which he had committed to memory.

Every passage he said seemed to him a volume. He truly felt the power of God's word.

This whole Island calls loudly for evangelical labor, but the mines the loudest. This is also the most important. Individuals here brought under the influence of the gospel, return to their homes throughout the Island, and carry with them an influence for *truth*.

I am persuaded more and more that any effort made by the church of Christ on behalf of this Island will not be regretted.

Whoever makes the greatest *sacrifice* now, will be the most *honoured* in time to come. God calls upon us to proceed and possess the land.

Rev. Joseph F. Kempton spent 8 weeks at Margaree and Mabou. Preached 16 sermons, attended 11 Prayer and Conference Meetings, visited 49 families, Baptized 4, Restored 1 to church fellowship, travelled 308 miles. Collected $58.07½.

Bro. Kempton labored under the direction of the Board for some years, first at Cow Bay, afterwards at the above mentioned places, and with much success.

Believing that God had called him to another field of labor, where the cause was self supporting, the Board reluctantly relinquished his services, and Bro. K. is now laboring successfully with the church at Lakeville, Kings Co.

Rev. E. C. Spinney is still engaged in Home Mission work at Cow Bay Mines and vicinity. Reports for 42½ weeks have been received. Preached 123 sermons, attended 170 Prayer and Conference Meetings, made 277 family visits, Baptized 11, distributed 2000 pages of tracts, travelled 1500 miles. Collected $229.45.

Extracts from letters.

June 21st, 1870.—"The cause is steadily increasing amidst all opposition. The words of Chillingworth 'The Bible the Bible only is the religion of Protestants' are being more needed now than formerly. We have been endeavouring to show what constitutes Christian baptism, and trust in some measure we have succeeded. Many who were previously blind as to the Scriptural teaching on this point now see. Error is rapidly being supplanted by the glorious truth of the Word of God.

Our meetings are interesting and well attended. The Sabbath Schools are engaging the attention of almost all, both old and young.

February 20th, 1871.—Since my last our church edifice at Cow Bay Mines has been completed, and opened for divine worship. So far as numbers are concerned; our most sanguine expectations have already been realized. On different occasions the House has been comfortably filled. There seems to be a great door opened for us which we hope will prove effectual.

March 29th.—The Lord is doing great things for us whereof we are glad. Christians have been and still are being revived. Some who had wandered very far from the fold, have come back with weeping. Sinners are awakening to a sense of their state before God. A few are awaiting baptism.

The *Christian Messenger* of 19th April published the following from Bro. Spinney. " Yesterday was a great day at Homeville, eight happy converts were buried with Christ in baptism and received into the fellowship of the Church. Others are anxious. Pray for us.

Rev. Jno. Shaw labored nine weeks and two days in the following places, Strait of Canso, West Bay, North Shore, Grand Ance, Kempt Road, Little Bras d'Or, North Sydney, South side North West Arm, the Bar, South Sydney, South Bar, Homeville, Cow Bay Mines, Glass Bay and Boularderie Island.

Preached 33 sermons, visited families, read the scriptures, remarked on the portions read, and prayed with them as often as I possible and conveniently could. Collected in aid of the Mission $81,64.

Congregations in general large and attentive, and in some instances broken down under the Word. Cape Breton is a great field already white to harvest. Among the Gaelic population in particular the Lord is working mightily, not through preaching exclusively, yet preaching (sermonizing) not excepted. The people meet themselves in private houses, read the Scriptures, exhort and pray together.

From Grand Mira to Sydney Mines, shore and backland settlement the work is going on. There may be some chaff and it is likely there is, but without a doubt the Lord of the harvest is gathering his wheat into the garner, and that through such means as he pleases, whether reading the Scriptures, exhortation, Ministerial or lay preaching (as people call it,) " The word of the Lord is not bound."

Rev. Alfred Chipman received an appointment of 13 weeks in destitute places adjacent to Sydney Town. The mission has only been partially fulfilled and therefore the statistics are not given in the report.

May 29th, Brother Chipman writes as follows: "At Victoria Coal Mines my principal station, no decided religious influence or activity, I regret to state, prevails. A few professors of religion connected with different churches reside there. All new coal mining centres are hard places for christian labor. Yet I shall watch anxiously for the opportunity to establish some other religious services than preaching, and I do hope the Lord will convert some souls there before your appointment closes. The attendance and attention at my present fort-nightly services are on the whole encouraging. At some other places where I have recently visited, the Spirit of the Lord was evidently working in some hearts. More than the foregoing statements I am not now in a position truthfully to make. "My word shall not return unto me void."

GUYSBOROUGH COUNTY.

Bro. Isaac Skinner, Licentiate, report of 8 weeks mission.

"I first went to Guysborough town; found the Church there without a pastor and much needing a shepherd to keep the flock together and impart to them the word of life.

Before visiting the Strait I went to New harbour on the Southern Shore and spent *eight* days. I was gladly received. Congregations were good and attentive, and a greater earnestness in the Cause of Christ was generally manifested.

On my arrival at the Strait I found that the little church at Sand Point had been for some time without the ministration of God's word and as is generally the case, the results were visible, in the cold state of the professed followers of Christ. I laboured praying that God would manifest himself in the hearts of those who had become indifferent, and produce a desire to return, as did the prodigal to the Father's house, and to influence those outside the fold of Christ to flee for refuge. I am pleased to state that in a small degree God did visit us by his grace and holy influence, by collecting together the little band of disciples, and giving them a desire to work together in harmony and love. Two young friends who had been awakened by the labors of Bro W. F. Armstrong last summer, came out in the full enjoyment of the religion of Jesus, and desired to follow their Redeemer in all his appointed ways.

Preached 20 sermons attended 18 Prayer and Conference Meetings, visited 60 families, tavelled 443 miles, collected $9.05.

COLCHESTER COUNTY.

Bro. G. O. Gates, Licentiate, having been assigned a mission of 8 weeks in New Annan, and the Head of Tatamagouche Bay, reported as follows:

"In both places I found regularly organized churches, but very small, and the love of many grown cold, "sheep without a Shepherd". The state of religion indeed appeared low, the lamp almost extinguished. Still a feeble few I found praying and hoping that yet a brighter day will dawn; trusting that though "sorrow may endure for the night, joy will come in the morning.

I was gladly received by the brethren, and was treated with uniform courtesy by all denominations. The field is a very inviting one. I left there many anxious souls, especially among the young.

In one of our social meetings a young man arose and requested prayer on his behalf. He informed me that he was tired of the ways of sin, found no pleasure in them and wanted to find Jesus as the Saviour of his soul. My prayer is that he may find that dear Redeemer. Two or three are waiting to join the Church at the earliest opportunity. " The waters are indeed being troubled."

In new Annan there are two quite prosperous Sabbath Schools. I visited them often and tried to encourage them. I trust the seed has been sown here, and that an abundant harvest will yet be gathered in. The work is the Lord's. He is able and also willing to bless. The people were very thankful to the Home Mission Board for remembering them and did cheerfully what they could in the way of remuneration.

I travelled 409 miles, preached 29 sermons, attended 13 Prayer and Conference Meetings, visited 106 families, some of them frequently, generally reading the Scriptures and offering prayer. Distributed 1230 pages of tracts; these were gladly received by all, and more than once have I been cheered by being informed of the comfort and encouragement derived from their perusal. " Cast thy bread upon the waters, and it shall be seen after many days." Collected in aid of the Mission $51.97.

CUMBERLAND COUNTY.

Rev. E. B. Corey has labored 13 weeks in the service of the Board.

Preached 60 sermons, attended 18 Prayer and Conference meetings, made 379 family visits, Baptized 10 persons distributed 2000 pages of tracts, travelled 500 miles, collected $40,89.

Extracts from letter of May 5th, " During my mission I have endeavoured to preach the gospel in the following

places, viz. Leicester, Mount Pleasant, Centreville, Port
Philip, Torry Bay, Goose River, Pugwash and Pugwash
River, Rail Road line Sec. No. 7.

In the month of March I labored at Torry Bay and Goose
River. The church was revived and strengthened, eight
happy converts were baptised upon a profession of their
faith in the Lord Jesus. Three were restored to the
fellowship of the Church.

In April I held special services at Pugwash River, some
mercy drops have fallen.

Two rejoicing converts were baptized in the presence of
many witnesses. A number more are expected. Our congregations are large and attentive, truly the Lord is displaying
his power in the salvation of sinners."

HANTS COUNTY.

Bro. Rufus Sanford, Licentiate, spent *seven* weeks at
Maitland and vicinity.

The following extract is a taken from a letter dated July
30th, 1870.

"I am pained to know that the little Baptist Church here
has been so destitute of ministerial labor for years past.
Revs. Geo. Wethers, and T. H. Porter, I think are the only
two who have expended labor here to any extent. The
interest as you may well suppose is very weak.

I am much encouraged in the work. The people seem
inclined to do all in their power to support the gospel in
their midst.

This field is one of deep interest and ought to receive
your special attention. If a missionary could be supported
in this place for one year, through the co-operation of the
Board with the people, and the blessing of God attending
his labors, I think that the cause would be self sustaining afterwards. There are many persons whom I found favourable to
Baptist sentiments. These need to meet the encouragement
arising from regular preaching services, a working organization.

My labors extended from Dimock Settlement to Noel,
inclusive, a distance of twenty miles. Within this
space I labored from house to house, reading the
Scriptures, with prayer, conversation and distribution
of tracts. We held two conference meetings, at the last of
which, two persons were received into the fellowship of the
church by letter. Also various matters neglected, respect-
ing the Church records, were arraigned; Bro. David
McCurdy was chosen Clerk, and a movement made in
reference to finishing the meeting house. May the Lord
prosper his work among those dear people."

Preached 20 sermons, attended 17 Prayer and Conference

meetings, made 120 family visits, distributed 683 pages of religious tracts, travelled 316 miles, 2 persons received into the church by letter, collected $41.92.

LUNENBURG COUNTY.

Mahone Bay, Lunenburg, North West. Rev. Augustus Shields labored in the service of the Board 8 weeks, preached 43 sermons, attended 7 Prayer and Conference meetings visited 120 families, distributed 420 pages of tracts, travelled 240 miles, collected $9.59.

On the 10th Feb. Bro. Shields wrote as follows: "I entered on the duties assigned me in Lunenburg County on the 20th Nov. Our brethren were happy to co-operate with me wherever I went. On week days I visited many places that otherwise would have been neglected. My heart was made glad in seeing many enquiring for "the way of life." I found it difficult to get a place in town; but in the Garden Lots, I preached to attentive, weeping hearers. I visited Heckman's Island several times.

We have a few believers there, they were glad of the privilege of hearing the precious gospel of Christ, and mourn that they are as Sheep without a fold, as there is no House of God in that place. I preached also at the Black Rocks."

The *Christian Messenger* of the 15th March contains a letter from Bro. Shields from which a few extracts have been gleaned.

"An unusual interest has been felt by the people in Mahone Bay and North West, for some weeks past. Last Sabbath I baptized *two* rejoicing souls, and expect to administer the sacred rite next Sabbath, as quite a number have obtained hope, and some received for membership.

The enemies of evangelical religion are mustering their forces to arrest the work. But how vain the attempt, since the work is evidently of the Lord! His conquering word has gone forth, and the impenitent are bowing before its power and majesty. May it everywhere go forth as brightness, and His salvation as a lamp that burneth, until all our churches are enlightened, refreshed and greatly strengthened.

Bro. Joseph Robbins, Licentiate spent *five* weeks at New Ross and made the following report dated 2nd Sept.

"I preached 20 sermons, held 7 Prayer and Conference meetings, made 60 family visits, distributed 1200 pages of tracts, travelled 240 miles, and collected $20 58½.

I found the little Church at New Ross feeble and somewhat cold, prayer and Conference meetings having been neglected during the winter, but I trust both will be sustained for the future.

The attention was very remarkable, and the congregations

constantly increased, on the last sabbath numbering *Eighty-five.* Baptst families in this settlement are few and widely scattered. There are many young people in this place in whose spiritual welfare I feel especially interested.

They are for the most part, thoughtful and some are enquiring the way to Zion. I found many families neglectful of family worship, and made it a particular part of my mission, strongly to urge parents to the performance of this important duty. There are two Sabbath Schools in connection with the Church, in both of which the young seem much interested.

May the Holy Spirit bless with power the word spoken in weakness, that saints may be revived, sinners converted, and God's name thereby glorified.

KING'S COUNTY.

Bro. Chas. Norwood, Lic., received an appointment of *six* weeks on Sherbrooke Road and Vicinity, and reports as follows :

" After a long time I have been enabled to fulfil the mission given me by the Board. The Lord has revived his cause wonderfully in that place—to Him be all the praise ; the work is still going on. I intend to labor there during the coming winter, I have been preaching about *five* years with considerable trials of mind, whether I could be the means under God of doing any good, but I now feel that the Lord has done great things for me whereof I am glad.

Oh for a faith that will not shrink, though pressed by every foe.

Rev. Jas. Parker wrote to the *Christian Messenger,* Nov. 30th, 1870, as follows :

" Bro. Chas. Norwood has been laboring for a few weeks on Beech Hill, a section of the third Horton Church assisted somewhat by Bro. C. Burguss of Windsor.

God has greatly blessed their labours. It was my privilege last Sabbath to baptize twelve young persons as the result of their labors, and the converting influence of the Spirit."

Preached 32 sermons, attended 19 prayer and Conference meetings, made 57 family visits, baptized 29, distributed 972 pages of tracts, travelled 220 miles, collected $13.98.

HANT'S COUNTY.

The following is from Rev. R. R. Philp :

MAITLAND. May 31st, 1871.

To the Secretary of the Nova Scotia Baptist Home Missionary Board.

DEAR BROTHER,—I feel very much encouraged in my missionary work in this place and vicinity. The Lord has graciously smiled upon us and owned our labours. Some years ago the brethren resolved in the strength of the Lord to build a house for his worship. They succeeded in completing the outside, but did nothing more until last Autumn when they concluded to have it finished. It required strong faith to attempt to finish the meeting house and at the same time aid in the support of a missionary yet they did attempt it and with the blessing of God their efforts proved successful. On the third Lord's day in May we enjoyed the pleasure of a visit from our brother the Rev. J. E. Goucher, pastor of North Baptist Church, Halifax, upon which occasion our meeting house was solemnly dedicated to God by prayer and praise, but the pleasure of the visit was made doubly joyous by the privilege of visiting the baptismal waters and burying with their Lord in baptism two happy believers. The day was delightfully fine a large number of spectators gathered at the water side, who manifested every token of respect while we attended to the solemn ordinance. In the prosecution of my work I have preached at the following places : Maitland, Upper a·d Lower Selmah, Noel and Noel Road. Fve mile River and Dimoch Settlement.

Yours truly,

R. R. PHILP.

ANTIGONISH COUNTY.

The following is from Rev. M. A. Bigelow :

ANTIGONISH, May 13, 1871.

Dear Brethren,—I have performed the Mission of six weeks appointed me on the South Shore last Summer. Had some good meetings. Trust the Spirit of God was with me and that good has been done.

Preached 30 time. Held 3 conference meetings, 14 prayer meetings. Made 40 family visits. Distributed 600 pages of tracts. Collected $11,00.

The people are poor. I have performed two months of the Mission appointed me in the Fall. Had some very interesting meetings, baptised 3. I am not well at present, hope I shall be able to finish the three months' mission before the Association.

Yours &c.,

M. A. BIGELOW.

Nova Scotia Home Missionary Society in account with D. McN'
P**R**, Treasurer.

1870.		Dr.	
June 14.	To Rev. R. R. Philp	$ 65 04
"	" Secretary for services	75 00
" ,	" " for Stationery and Postages	5 60
July 21.	" Rev. Wm. McPhee	60 00
"	" Rev. J. F. Kempton	5 93
"	" Rev. E. C. Spinney	1 25
"	" Stephen Selden	55 00
Sept. 2.	" G. O. Gates	3 50
"	" Rufus Sandford	5 38
" 6.	" Rev. M. A. Bigelow	26 00
"	" Isaac Skinner	38 95
"	" Joseph H. Robins	11 41
Oct. 6.	" Isaac Skinner	12 00
"	" Rev. Wm. McPhee	55 00
Nov. 25.	" Rev. E. C. Spinney	40 00
Dec. 17.	" Rev. Wm. McPhee	55 00
"	" Rev. John Shaw	21 44
1871.		
Jan. 21.	" Rev. R. R. Philp	50 00
"	" Charles Norwood	28 02
Mar. 3.	" Rev. Wm. McPhee	55 00
"	" Rev. Augustus Shields	50 91
"	" Rev. E. C. Spinney	38 55
May 31.	" Rev. E. C. Spinney	50 20
"	" Balance	374 25
		$1179 43

1870-		Cr.	
June 1.	By Cash in hand	$211 94
July 5.	" Cash from Coupons	30 00
" 16.	" Central Association	314 23
Aug. 31.	" Miss Sophia Bishop	1 00
Sept. 2.	" H. C. Creed (Yarmouth)	10 00
Oct. 11.	" J. W. Barss per Rev. D., Tupper $50 less 28 cents paid for Postage and Post Office Order	40 72
" 21.	" George Frail per S. Selden	2 00
Nov. 2.	" Rev. Dr. Cramp	10 00
Dec. 23.	" By Eastern Association	342 36
1871.		
Jan. 16.	" Judge McCully	50 00
Feb. 11.	" 1st. Horton Church	50 00
" 15.	" Granville Street Church, (Halifax)	66 37
Mar. 16.	" Week of Prayer Offering per S. Selden	5 00
" 21.	" 1st. Cornwallis Church per R. N. Beckwith	7 87
" 25.	" A friend per Rev. Dr. Cramp	10 00
April 5.	" Winkworth Chipman per R. N. Beckwith	4 00
" 20.	" Rev. John Shaw returned	14 94
		$1179 43
June 1.	" Balance on hand	374 25

Audited and found correct }
JOHN STEELE. }

Contributions.

ARICHAT.

(Collected by Rev. Wm. McPhee.

Mrs. Chandler	$3 00
Collection	3 00
Mrs. Chandler	3 40
John Bew	2 00
Annie Bew	1 00
Wm. Chandler, Esq.	1 30

$12 70

WEST BAY.

H. McKinnon and family	$2 00
John Morrison	1 12
Malcolm McLeod	0 75
J. N. Brown	14 50
N. McIntyre	1 00
Angus McLeod	1 00
Peter Paint, Jr.	5 00
Walter Flynn	1 00
Collection	4 00
Peter McFarlane	0 75
Ewen McKinnon	2 00
Mrs. Angus McLeod	2 70
Widow McLeod	0 20
Collection	2 50
Do.	5 50
Do.	3 00

$43 72

ST. ANN'S.

Christopher McLeod	$0 50
John McKuy	0 80
Roderick McLeod	2 25
Collection's at St.Ann's,Baddeck.	18 50
At St. Ann's, Baddeck	7 00
Collection and donations at Cow Bay	20 50
At Big Glace Bay	4 50
At North Sydney	8 00

$26 05

(Collected by Charles Norwood.)

Mrs. Jacob Stephens	$0 25
Nathan Ward	0 12
Mrs. Leander Schofile	0 13
Jacob Stephens	0 50
John McDonald	0 50
Benjamin Piers	0 62
James Ward	0 25
Alfred Smith	0 25
Aaron Ward	0 25
Wm. Ward	0 25
Wm. Webster	0 25
Edgar Webster	0 28
Roxana Jones	0 50
Fanny De Winter	0 50
Piers Loyd	0 50
James Dodge	0 14
Sophia Walton	0 25
James Turner	0 25
Enoch Dodge	0 50
Thadens Walton	0 25
Eliza A. Wood	0 12
William Morton	0 25
Charles Jones	0 25
Thomas Jones	0 25
Thomas Jarvis	0 25
Wm. Lockhart	0 50
Mrs. William Lockhart	0 25

Nelson Lockhart	$0 12
Mrs. T. Walton	0 25
Mr. Jarvis	0 50
Charles Jarvis	0 12
Miss McGee	0 25
Thomas Walton	0 25
Mr. Lautz	0 62
Miss Butler	0 12
Mrs. J. Butler	0 50
Mrs. Charles Jarvis	0 25
Mrs. Thomas Jones	0 25
Mrs. Lucilla Jarvis	0 25
Edward Try	0 12
Thomas Lockhart	0 25
Collection	1 57

$13 98

NEW ANNAN.

(Collected by G. O. Gates.)

Collection	$5 59
Deacon A. Conkey	1 00
Deacon Wm. Cutten	1 50
Miss Rachel Downing*	4 00
Mr. Daniel Fields	3 25
Mrs. James Wilson	0 50
Mr. David Wilson	1 50
Mr. John Wilson	0 62
Mr. Robert Wilson	0 75
Mrs. George Shearer	1 00
Mrs. Peter Hynds	0 50
Miss Annie Cox	0 45
Mr. John Tucker	0 50
Mr. Charles Wortman	0 50
Mr. W. M. Murdoch	0 50
Mrs. John Cox	0 50
Mrs. John Murphy	0 25
Mr. Hugh McKay	0 25
Mr. William Drysdale	1 00
Mr. Robert Kent	3 00
Miss Morrison	1 00
Mr. A. Swan	0 50
Mr. M. Scott	0 25
A Friend	2 00
Miss Lynds	1 00
Mrs. A. Tucker	0 75
Mrs. George Cox	0 50
Mr. George Nelson	1 50

$34 06

*Miss D. also gave your Missionary
$3 for Foreign Missions.

HEAD OF TATAMAGOUCHE BAY.

Collections	$2 02
Mr. George Slade	1 00
Miss J. Spinney	0 62
Miss E. Dunphy	0 50
Miss Jane Spinney	0 50
Mr. Joseph Harrington	1 00
Mrs. Henry Roberts	0 50
Mrs. William Matatate	0 50
Mrs. William Holmes	0 50
Mr. Henry Roberts	1 00
Mr. Joshua Slade	2 00
Mr. Ephraim Slade	1 00
Mr. Edward Munro	0 50
Mr. Samuel Wetherbie	1 00
Mr. Daniel Goodwin	1 00
Mr. Joseph Roberts	0 25

Mr. Thos. Shade	$0 25
Mr. Thos. Roberts	1 00
Mr. John Shade	1 00
Mrs. Thomas Roberts	0 25
	$17 29

NEW HARBOUR.
(Collected by Isaac Skinner, Lic.)

Mrs. Andrew Songster	$1 00
Miss Jane O'Hara	1 00
Joseph Luddington	0 25
Mrs. Wm. A. Sangster	0 50
Adam G. Sangster	0 20
Mrs. G. Sangster	0 12
Thomas Luddington	0 40
John O'Hara	0 25
Robert Sangster	0 25
Edward O'Hara	0 50
Miss F. C. Sangster	0 25
Mrs. Joseph Sangster	0 12
	$4 85

SAND POINT.

Mrs. Caroline Summers	$1 00
S. Summers	0 25
Mrs. Turlet	0 50
Mrs. Annie Turlet	0 20
Richard Reid	0 25
Miss Rebecca Carter	0 25
Miss Mary Jane Silver	0 25
Miss Margaret Saint	0 12
Miss Margaret Shepherd	0 12
Miss Susan Grant	0 25
Miss Catherine L. Grant	0 25
Richard B. Carrigan	0 50
Mrs. B. Carrigan	0 25
	$4 20

(Collected by Rev. M. A. Biglow.)

Mrs. John Bowden	$1 00
Alexander Bowden	0 25
Susan Bowden	0 25
Harriet Bowden	0 25
Fred Bowden	0 25
Joseph Pravon	0 25
Allen L. Pravon	0 25
Samuel Pravon	0 25
Caroline Pravon	0 12
Jeremiah Pravon	0 25
Edward Pravon	0 12
Maria Pravon	0 12
Joseph Ash	0 25
Hannah Ash	0 12
Charles Ash	0 12
Mrs. C. Ash	0 12
John Ash	0 25
Margaret Ash	0 12
Peter Reddie	0 25
Ellen Reddie	0 12
Jennet Reddie	0 12
Mary Reddie	0 12
Mary C. Reddie	0 12
Abe Ash	0 25
Joseph Celvie	0 25
Ann Celvie	0 12
Thomas Shepherd	0 25
Mrs. T. Shepherd	0 12
Joseph Disman	0 25
William Disman	0 25
C. Ann Disman	0 12
Frank Disman	0 25
Jane Disman	0 25
Rebecca Disman	0 25
George Douglass	0 25
Susan Elms	0 12
Mary Elms	0 50
Harriet Fee	0 50

Matthew Day	$0 25
Charles Paris	0 25
Catherine Elms	0 25
Mrs. A. Reddie	0 12
A Friend	0 17
Collection	2 20
	$12 12

(Collected by Rev. E. B. Corey.)

Wallace	$1 20
Goose River	13 63
Leicester	1 56
Wm. Hunter	1 67
Pugwash	4 00
Pugwash River	4 00
Mount Pleasant Centerville Ch.	16 00
	$40 89

(Collected by Rev. Jos. H. Robbins.)

George Blown	$1 00
Emeline Brown	0 25
Mary Brown	0 25
John Reese	0 25
Newton Brown	0 25
Gilbert Brown	0 25
David Reese	0 25
David Brown	0 25
Samuel Brown	1 00
Joseph Lantz	0 37
Peter Lantz	0 50
Wm. Brown	0 50
James Lantz	0 75
Mrs. H. Lewis	0 12
Henry Brown	1 00
David Brown	0 75
Geo. Collins	0 62
Geo. Elliot	1 00
Jacob Rafuse	0 50
Wm. Corkum	0 80
Geo. Meister	1 00
Wm. Meister	0 75
David Corkum	0 25
Rufus Corkum	0 25
Edward O'Neill	1 00
Elias Bezanson	0 50
Wm. Bezanson	0 37
Silas Lantz	0 25
Fred. Lantz	0 25
Samuel Turner	0 25
Hannah Lantz	0 12
Collection	4 01
	$20 59

(Collected by Rufus Sandford, Lic.)

Mr. James Burgess	$2 50
Capt. Daniel Campbell	5 00
Mrs. Daniel Campbell	2 50
Mr. L. B. Cochran	0 50
Mr. Rupert Cox	0 50
Mr. Benjamin Dimock	1 00
Collection at Dimock Settlement	0 30
" Rockville	2 42
" Noel	1 70
" Selma	6 55
Mr. Alex. Gillis	5 00
Mr. George Smith	5 00
Mr. David McCurdy	5 00
Mrs. Robert Monteith	1 00
Mr. John McDonald	1 50
Mr. Finlay McDonald	0 50
Mr. S. B. Whiston	0 50
Mr. Robert Smith	0 25
Friends	0 19
	$41 92

MIRA.

(Collected by Rev. E. C. Spinney.)

Nehemiah Martell	$7 00
Deacon Charles Martell	5 00
Philip Spencer	4 00
A. J. Spencer	4 00
Edward Dickson	4 00
Pernenus Spencer	4 00
John Nicoll	4 00
Timothy Spencer	3 00
Wentworth Spencer	2 50
William Dickson	1 50
Samuel Dickson	1 50
Edward Spencer	2 00
David Phillips	1 00
Caleb Huntington	4 00
Alex. McDonald	1 00
John Dillon	1 00
Ed. Peters	1 00
Nathan Spencer	1 00
Charles Spencer, Senr.	1 00
Charles Spencer, Junr.	1 00
Geo. Dickson, Junr.	0 75
William Peters	0 50
James Nicoll	1 00
Mrs. Charles Martell	1 00
Mrs. John Nicoll	1 00
Mrs. William Dickson	1 00
Mrs. Charles Spencer, Senr.	0 50
Mrs. Edward Spencer	0 50
Mrs. Philip Spencer	0 50
Mrs. Charles Spencer, Junr.	1 00
Patience J. Martell	4 00
Louise Martell	1 00
Emma Martell	0 50
Sarah Nicoll	0 70
Annie Nicoll	0 70
Alice Nicoll	0 50
Marcilla Spencer	0 50
James Spencer	0 50
Clara Spencer	0 25
Maggie Spencer	0 50
Laleah Spencer	0 50
Mrs. David Phillips	0 50
Collections	2 44

HOMEVILLE.

Stetson Holmes	$10 00
Joseph Holmes	0 25
Deacon Arnold Holmes	4 00
William Holmes Senr.	4 00
Collected by Thos. Martell	5 25
Geo. Martell	1 25
Arnold Holmes, Junr.	0 50
Joseph Hart, Little Baddeck	5 00
Mrs. Galen Holmes	7 00
Mrs. Arnold Holmes, Senr.	1 50
Mrs. Geo. Dillon	1 50
Mrs. Joseph Holmes	1 25
Mrs. John Martell	1 00
Mrs. Geo. Martell	1 00
Mrs. Arnold Holmes, Junr.	1 00
Mrs. Thos. Peach	0 50
Mrs. William Holmes	0 25
Mrs. Charles Martell	0 25
Mrs. Thos. Martell	0 25
Mrs. E. Balbin	0 50
Annie E. Holmes	5 00
Amelia Holmes	0 75

Julia Martell	$0 50
Clarinda D. Soverance	0 50
Elvenia Holmes	0 50
Caroline Martell	0 25
Esther Martell	0 25
Lizzie Holmes	0 12
Mrs. Arnold Martell, Little Glace Bay	1 00
William Holmes, Junr.	1 00

SOUTH HEAD.

Deacon Charles Shepard	$4 50
Seth Shepard	4 00
Charles Peters	3 00
John Murrant, Junr.	2 00
William Murrant, Junr.	2 00
B. Shepard, Esq.	1 50
Edward Murrant	1 50
Mrs. Seth Shepard	1 50
Mrs. B. Shepard	1 50
Mrs. M. McInnis	0 25
Mrs. Joel Shepard	0 25
Mrs. Anthony Murrant	0 25
Mrs. Joel Peters	0 50
Mrs. Wentworth Peters	0 25
Annie C. Shepard	0 50
Elizabeth Shepard	0 25
Mary Ann Murrant	0 50
Louisa Murrant	0 10
Minnie Shepard	0 50
Orilla Murrant	0 06
Maggie McKenzie	0 25

COW BAY MINES.

Deacon S. E. Peters	$13 50
R. D. Rice	9 50
O. J. Spencer	9 50
Jos. W. Peppett	10 00
John McPhall	5 75
Roderick McDonald	3 00
Charles McDonald	2 00
Alex. McPhall	2 00
Albert Shepherd	2 50
Henry Morley	2 00
William Shepherd, Sr.	2 50
Andrew Fletcher	1 00
David Stacy	1 25
Mrs. S. E. Peters	2 00
" R. D. Rice	2 00
" Charles Inman	2 00
" William Shepherd, Sr.	1 00
" Alice Woods	1 00
" John Powers	1 00
Mrs. Albert Shepherd	$0 60
" Andrew Fletcher	0 25
Sarah Woods	2 00
Mary Ann Welton	1 00
Margaret McDonald	1 50
Jane Shepherd	0 40
Elizabeth McLean	0 25
Annie McDonald	0 25
Sarah McPhall	0 25
George Scott	1 50
	$249 92

NOTE.—A portion of the foregoing were received after the close of the preceding year.

R. N. B.

CONSTITUTION

N. S. BAPTIST HOME MISSIONARY SOCIETY.

I. This Society shall be called " The Nova Scotia Baptist Home Missionary Society."

II. The object of this Society shall be the preaching of the Gospel throughout Nova Scotia, and Newfoundland, the assistance of feeble Churches, and the planting of new ones.

III. Any person may become a member of this Society by contributing five shillings and upwards annually, to its funds. Any person contributing five pounds at one time shall be a Life Member. Any person contributing twenty pounds at one time, or whose contributions shall amount to that sum, shall be a Life Director. Every Association or Auxiliary, which contributes annually to this Society shall be entitled to be represented by one Delegate for every five pounds so contributed; and every Baptist Church contributing annually to the funds of the Society, shall have the privilege of sending a delegate. Should the funds so contributed exceed five pounds, such church shall be entitled to send one delegate for every five pounds contributed,—*Provided;* That no Association, Auxiliary or Church, shall be entitled to send more than five Delegates at one time.

IV. The officers of this Society shall be a President, Vice-Presidents, Secretary, Treasurer, and Auditor, who shall be annually appointed by the Society from among its members.

V. The Society shall annually appoint a Board of Management, consisting of twenty-four members, members of Baptist Churches, seven of whom shall reside in the place designated, from year to year, as the location of the Board, or in its neighborhood, and five shall constitute a quorum. The officers above named shall be *ex-officio* members of the Board. The following shall be the duties of the Board, viz.:—To meet from time to time for the despatch of business, due notice of such meeting being given; to appoint missionaries, and assign their respective spheres of labor; to expend the funds for the objects of the Society, provided that all amounts contributed for any specific purpose shall be faithfully applied as far as possible in accordance with the wishes of the donors; to employ agents for the collection of funds, and for the general advancement of the interests of the Society; and to furnish a report of the proceedings of the past year at the Annual meeting.

VI. Every Auxiliary Society which shall agree to commit all its funds to the direction of this Society, shall be entitled to receive Missionary labor in such field as it may designate, to an amount at least equal to its contributions; provided that such designation be intimated at the time of payment.

VII. The members of Auxiliary Societies shall be members of this Society. Life Directors shall be entitled to attend and vote at meetings of the Board.

VIII. The Annual meeting of the Society shall be held at such time and place as shall be determined upon at a previous Annual meeting. At that meeting, the officers of the Society for the ensuing year shall be appointed, and such other business transacted as the members then present deem expedient.

IX. No alteration of this Constitution shall be made without an affirmative vote of two-thirds of the members present at an annual meeting.

BYE LAWS

OF THE

N. S. BAPTIST HOME MISSIONARY BOARD.

ARTICLE 1.—This Board shall meet for the dispatch of business vt 4 o'clock, P. M., on the 1st Wednesday of each month,—Also at such other times as duly called by the Chairman, or Secretary, or two other members of the Board.

ARTICLE 2.—Each meeting of the Board shall be opened and closed with prayer, and the minutes of preceding meetings read and approved.

ARTICLE 3.—None but Licentiates from regular Baptist Churches and ordained Ministers, recognized as such by a regular Baptist Association, shall be employed as Missionaries for the Society.

ARTICLE 4.—No Missionary shall be at liberty to change his field of labor or to extend the time of his service beyond appointment without consent of the Board.

ARTICLE 5.—The compensation allowed, generally, for married, and ordained Missionaries shall be eight dollars per week, for married licentiates and unmarried ordained Missionaries seven dollars, for unmarried licentiates six dollars, in each case exclusive of travelling expenses.

ARTICLE 6.—All Missionaries or pastors serving under the Board are empowered and expected to make all reasonable effort during the time, and in the localities of such service, to collect funds in aid of the Treasury, to be transmitted forthwith to the same, or reported to the Board, credited towards labor performed.

ARTICLE 7.—On the expiration of Missions, reports shall be promptly made to the Board, by Missionaries, stating definitely, the number of weeks' service, number of sermons preached, visits made, miles travelled, pages of tracts distributed, baptisms performed Sabbath Schools visited, other meetings attended, Churches, Sabbath Schools, Temperance Societies and prayer meetings organized; moneys and other contributions, with the names of the donors ; and such other facts connected with their labors likely to be of general interest.

ARTICLE 8.—No moneys shall be paid by the Treasurer, except on an order signed by the Chairman and Secretary.

ARTICLE 9.—The Chairman and Secretary shall sign no orders for moneys from the Treasury unless for accounts checked by the Auditors.

ARTICLE 10.—No accounts shall be audited until ordered by the Board.

ARTICLE 11.—The Board shall not accept and submit accounts to the Auditors, unless presenting full particulars of debits and credits, &c., as specified in Article 7.

ARTICLE 12.—The Secretary of this Board, with the consent of the Editor of the *Christian Messenger*, shall furnish, monthly, for publication in that paper, the following items, viz:—Letters received [during the month], appointments made, amount of funds in the Treasury, amounts due Missionaries, the names of Missionaries and their fields of labor, members of the Board present at last meeting, and such other particulars as may be ordered by the Board.

ARTICLE 13.—A copy of these Bye Laws shall be forwarded by the Secretary to each missionary on his appointment.